Jan van Eyck: Two Paintings of
Saint Francis Receiving the Stigmata

J.R.J. van Asperen de Boer

Kenneth Bé

Marigene H. Butler

Peter Klein

Katherine Crawford Luber

Joseph J. Rishel

Maurits Smeyers

James Snyder

Carlenrica Spantigati

This book was published with the assistance of the Getty Grant Program.
It was also supported by an endowment fund for scholarly publications
established by grants from CIGNA Foundation and
the Andrew W. Mellon Foundation at the Philadelphia Museum of Art.

Jan van Eyck:
Two Paintings of
Saint Francis
Receiving
the Stigmata

PHILADELPHIA MUSEUM OF ART

Copyright 1997 Philadelphia Museum of Art
Produced by the Department of Publications and Graphics
Philadelphia Museum of Art
Benjamin Franklin Parkway at Twenty-sixth Street
P.O. Box 7646
Philadelphia, PA 19101-7646

Edited by Jane Watkins, with the assistance of Curtis Scott
Production Manager: Sandra Klimt
Design concept by Richard Hendel
Layout by Ink, Inc., New York
Translation of Carlenrica Spantigati's essay by
    John R. Shepley
Printed by Amilcare Pizzi, S.p.A., Milan

Library of Congress Cataloging-in-Publication Data
Eyck, Jan van, 1390–1441
    Jan van Eyck: Two paintings of Saint Francis receiving
the stigmata / J.R.J. van Asperen de Boer ... [et al.].
        p.   cm.
    Includes bibliographical references and index.
    ISBN 0-87633-115-0 (alk. paper).
    1. Eyck, Jan van, 1390–1441. Saint Francis receiving the
stigmata. 2. Panel painting, Flemish—Attribution. 3. Panel
painting, Flemish—Expertising. 4. Francis, of Assisi, Saint,
c. 1181–1226—Art. 5. Philadelphia Museum of Art.
6. Galleria Sabauda (Turin, Italy). I. Asperen de Boer,
J.R.J. van. II. Title.
ND673.E9A75 1997   97-17147
759.9493—DC21   CIP

Printed and bound in Italy

Contents

Jan van Eyck's Two Paintings of
Saint Francis Receiving the Stigmata

The Philadelphia and Turin versions are
reproduced actual size on the following pages

2 color
Photocopies

Pl. II. Jan van Eyck,
*Saint Francis of Assisi
Receiving the Stigmata*,
1430s, oil on panel,
11½ x 13⅛"
(29.2 x 33.4 cm),
Galleria Sabauda,
Turin, cat. 187.
Reproduced actual
size.

Preface

In February 1983, at the annual meeting of the College Art Association held that year in Philadelphia, Kenneth Craig of Boston College prepared a session on what was essentially a local topic: the painting *Saint Francis of Assisi Receiving the Stigmata* attributed to Jan van Eyck, housed at the Philadelphia Museum of Art as part of the John G. Johnson Collection. The speakers were four in number: Marigene H. Butler, Head of Conservation at the Philadelphia Museum of Art; James Snyder of Bryn Mawr College; Kenneth Bé, a geologist with a special interest in Flemish paintings who is now a conservator at the Cleveland Museum of Art, and Joseph J. Rishel, Senior Curator of European Painting before 1900 and the John G. Johnson Collection. It proved to be a remarkably stimulating session and served as a foundation for thoroughly investigating this enigmatic work and its relationship to the larger but nearly identical version in the Galleria Sabauda, Turin. At the Philadelphia Museum of Art the incentive to do what had long been discussed took form: to properly clean the picture, which had not been treated in depth since the restoration by Roger Fry in 1906, after Johnson acquired the picture. Marigene Butler's conservation of Philadelphia's diminutive masterpiece has revealed a considerable body of new information now published here. Most importantly for this project, she became, through her growing knowledge of this particular work, an international spokesperson for the investigation of the technique and materials of Van Eyck paintings. Happily, the Philadelphia investigation soon found collaboration in Italy, where similar work was in process on the Turin *Saint Francis*.

Much time has passed since that collegial set of discussions in 1983 and much new information has been gathered. The staff of the Galleria Sabauda in Turin have been tremendously generous in sharing their discoveries made during the conservation of their beautiful picture. We are delighted that Carlenrica Spantigati, then director of the Galleria Sabauda, Turin, now Soprintendente of the Soprintendenza per i Beni Artistici e Storici del Piemonte, has been able to contribute an essay to this anthology, offering a point of view that balances our perspective. Of equal importance is Mrs. Butler's collaboration with Professor J.R.J. van Asperen de Boer on the examination with infrared reflectography of the Turin picture and the remarkable illuminated manuscript pages from the Turin-Milan Hours preserved at the Museo Civico d'Arte Antica in Turin, allowing for the first time an unprecedented comparison of the underdrawing of these works. Professor Maurits Smeyers has provided his own observations on the Turin-Milan Hours and their relationship to the two Saint Francis pictures. Professor Peter Klein has carried out dendrochronological analyses of the two panels.

It is to Marigene Butler that this project owes its vitality, and this book, published in the year of her retirement from the Philadelphia Museum of Art, bears witness to her contributions to the life of the Museum during her nineteen-year tenure as Head Conservator. Documented here is the wealth of information and opinion that she has been able to gather to date. Scores of people have generously assisted Mrs. Butler in her research and openly shared their opinions with us. Most happily, the line isolating the history of art from clinical investigation, so often relegated to an appendix of an art-historical discussion of a problem such as this, soon blurred.

The one great sadness marking our work was the death of James Snyder in 1990. His unwavering faith in the transcendent and profoundly poetic genius of Jan van Eyck is documented in his essay, reproduced here essentially as it was presented at the College Art Association in 1983. Following that session, he was able to observe Mrs. Butler's restoration of the picture and encourage new lines of investigation very actively for several years.

We are grateful for the patience and beneficence of several sponsors whose belief in the importance of scholarship to the mission of the Museum sustained this project over many years. This book was published with the generous assistance of the Getty Grant Program and was supported by an endowment fund for scholarly publications established by grants from CIGNA Foundation and the Andrew W. Mellon Foundation at the Philadelphia Museum of Art.

These essays are by no means presented as a definitive answer to the various thorny questions surrounding these two pictures. The complex problems of their relationship to Jan van Eyck himself and their place in the development of fifteenth-century Flemish painting in general continue to hold many mysteries. Our task has been not to persuade but to clarify the state of the problem as it now stands, to provide through new scientific evidence a broader and richer platform from which to view these two beautiful objects, and, we hope, to prompt fresh thoughts on the nature of Jan van Eyck, his studio, and his far-ranging influence.

Anne d'Harnoncourt
The George D. Widener Director

Joseph J. Rishel
Senior Curator of European Painting before 1900 and the John G. Johnson Collection

Joseph J. Rishel

The Philadelphia and Turin Paintings: The Literature and Controversy over Attribution

The small painting *Saint Francis of Assisi Receiving the Stigmata* is one of the most celebrated pictures from the collection of Philadelphia lawyer John G. Johnson (1840–1917), housed since 1932 in the Philadelphia Museum of Art (pl. I). Purchased in 1894 by Johnson in London, it was soon acknowledged as a masterpiece, one of the most important things of its kind to cross the Atlantic.[1] Since then, the painting and its relationship to the strikingly similar version in the Galleria Sabauda, Turin (pl. II), have attracted a diversity of opinions nearly unprecedented in the study of Flemish Primitives, itself one of the most densely researched aspects of European art history. The bibliography on the two pictures is huge; a selected bibliography is included in this volume to outline the range of opinions surrounding the works, giving some idea of the attraction these pictures hold and the problems they continue to pose for many connoisseurs and scholars. Our purpose here is to review the physical history of the Philadelphia picture, to restate some of the essential facts about it that have not been called into question, to comment on some of the critical opinions concerning its attribution and its place in the production of Jan van Eyck and his workshop, and to draw some sharper comparisons with its sister in Turin.

Like the Turin picture, the modern history of the Johnson painting can be taken back only to the early nineteenth century. A Scotsman, William à Court (1779–1860), held the crucial post of British envoy to Portugal from 1824 to 1828.[2] It may have been in connection with his departure from Lisbon when he was transferred to St. Petersburg to negotiate the British position in the Russo-Turkish war that he wrote to his brother in London concerning the safe storage and shipment of his possessions, particularly his collection of pictures. His brother's response from London, dated March 9, 1827, suggests that his belongings had already arrived from Portugal: "I saw Planta on the subject of your pictures; he seemed to think it would be better to leave them in the Custom House 'til your arrival. Since this I find the duties will not amount to more than £4 or 5. I therefore shall pay it without troubling Planta further on the subject."[3] Unfortunately, no specific list of paintings survives from that correspondence. It was only in 1843, by which time he had become the first Lord Heytesbury, that William à Court

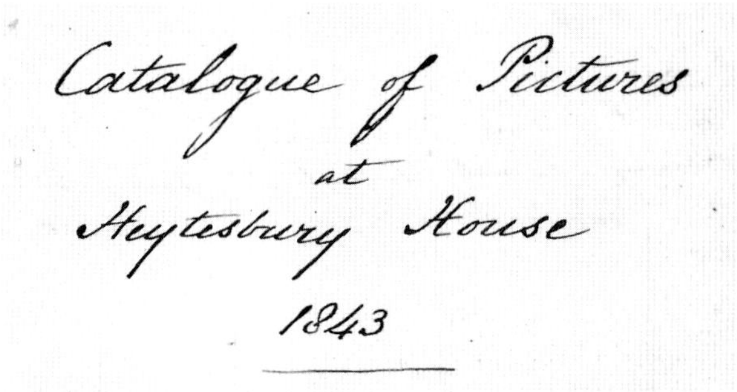

Catalogue of Pictures at Heytesbury House 1843

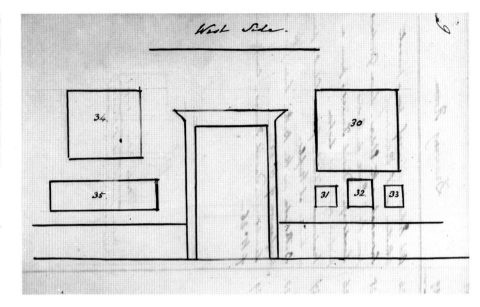

West Side.

drew up an inventory of the pictures then in his country place, Heytesbury House (Wiltshire), supplementing his lists with detailed outline drawings of how the works were arranged on his walls (figs. 1, 2). Hung just to the right of the door on the west wall of his drawing room was a small picture annotated as "St. Francis–Albrecht Dürer from a physician at Lisbon" (fig. 3). In 1955 the new Baron Heytesbury confirmed that the inventory was indeed in his great-grandfather's hand, supporting the Lisbon connection. In an addendum to the inventory giving the cost of each of the seventy-six works in the house, the *Saint Francis* is quoted at £8, one of the lowest amounts placed on the items listed (fig. 4).[4]

It was at Heytesbury House that the inveterate German tourist and connoisseur G. F. Waagen saw the work, publishing it in 1857 in his fourth, supplemental volume on collections in Great Britain as by Jan van Eyck, noting its close comparison to the Dresden triptych, and speculating that it may date from the time of Jan's diplomatic mission to Portugal in 1428–29 for Philip the Good, Duke of Burgundy.[5] The painting was exhibited in 1865 at the British Institution, London, as by Jan van Eyck, an attribution reiterated in 1886, when it was shown at the Royal Academy.[6] It was at this point that heated debate on its authorship commenced.

As Baron Heytesbury noted in 1955, his family's interest in the picture waned after the death of his great-grandfather. The panel was sold from Heytesbury House on November 14, 1894, to the London firm of Gooden and Fox for £300; Mr. Johnson purchased it from them a month later for £700. Johnson bequeathed his entire collection to the City of Philadelphia, and the picture has been on almost constant public view since his death in 1917.

Following its second London showing, comment was made on the poor condition of certain passages, particularly in the robes of Brother Leo and the addition at the top.[7] This addition, along with a considerable amount of overpaint,

was removed by Johnson's close friend and advisor Roger Fry when he restored the picture in New York in 1906 (fig. 5).[8]

Concerning the earlier history of the picture, there is a rare, if enigmatic, document first published in 1860 by Alexandre Pinchart.[9] On February 10, 1470, before his departure for a trip to the Holy Land, Anselme Adornes (1424–1483), the eldest son of a wealthy family of Genoese merchants who had been established in Bruges since the late fourteenth century, drew up a will, known through a transcription (fig. 6). The relevant passage reads: "Item, I give to each of my dear daughters, to be theirs, to wit, Marguerite, Carthusian, and Louise, Sint-Truiden, a picture wherein Saint Francis in portraiture from the hand of Master Jan van Eyck, and make the condition that in the shutters of the same little pictures be made my likeness and that of my wife, as well as can be made."[10]

W. H. James Weale, in 1886, seems to have been the first to connect this document with the Heytesbury picture, which he had just seen at the Royal Academy, and the very similar (albeit four times larger) *Saint Francis Receiving the Stigmata*, which had been in the Royal Gallery, Turin, since 1866.[11] He observed further that the pictures could not have been painted by the hand of Jan van Eyck directly for Anselme Adornes, as the latter would have been only fifteen years old at the time of Jan's death in 1441.[12] Weale also speculated on the brown habit of the saint and the black habit worn by the Franciscan lay brothers, which he stated were not introduced into the Low Countries prior to the end of the fifteenth century (the gray friars predominating until then), and concluded

Fig. 1. Heytesbury House inventory of pictures compiled by the first Lord Heytesbury in 1843.

Fig. 2. Lord Heytesbury's outline drawing of the west wall of the drawing room, 1843, with the Philadelphia *Saint Francis* as number 31.

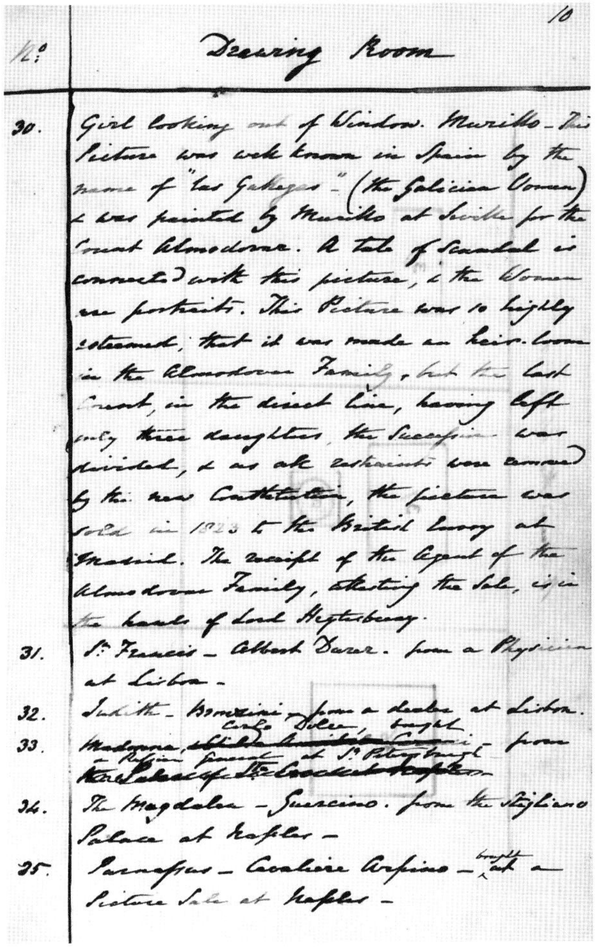

10

No. Drawing Room

30. Girl looking out of Window. Murillo – This Picture was well known in Spain by the name of "las Gallegas" – (the Galician Women) & was painted by Murillo at Seville for the Count Almodovar. A tale of Scandal is connected with this picture, & the Women are portraits. This Picture was so highly esteemed, that it was made an heir-loom in the Almodovar Family, but the last Count, in the direct line, having left only three daughters, the succession was divided, & as all entailments were annulled by the new Constitution, the picture was sold in 1823 to the British Envoy at Madrid. The receipt of the Agent of the Almodovar Family, attesting the sale, is in the hands of Lord Heytesbury.

31. St. Francis – Albert Durer. from a Physician at Lisbon –

32. Judith – Bronzini – from a dealer at Lisbon.

33. ~~Madonna [illegible]~~ Carlo Dolci, bought [illegible] at St. Petersburgh – from [illegible]

34. The Magdalen – Guercino. from the Stigliano Palace at Naples –

35. Parnassus – Cavaliere Arpino – bought at a Picture Sale at Naples –

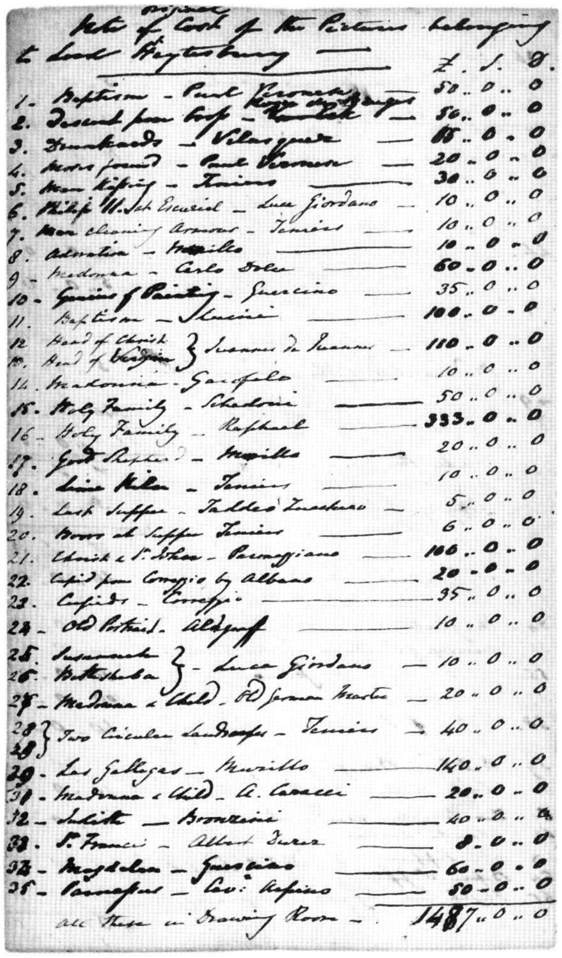

Note of original Cost of the Pictures belonging to Lord Heytesbury —

		£. s. d.
1.	Baptism – Paul Veronese	50 .. 0 .. 0
2.	Descent from Cross – [illegible]	50 .. 0 .. 0
3.	Drunkards – Velasquez	85 .. 0 .. 0
4.	[illegible] – Paul Veronese	20 .. 0 .. 0
5.	[illegible] – Teniers	30 .. 0 .. 0
6.	Philip II. at the Escurial – Luca Giordano	10 .. 0 .. 0
7.	Man cleaning Armour – Teniers	10 .. 0 .. 0
8.	Adoration – Murillo	10 .. 0 .. 0
9.	Madonna – Carlo Dolce	60 .. 0 .. 0
10.	Genius of Painting – Guercino	35 .. 0 .. 0
11.	Baptism – Sacchi	100 .. 0 .. 0
12. 13.	Head of Christ / Head of Virgin } Juanes de Juanes	110 .. 0 .. 0
14.	Madonna – Garofalo	10 .. 0 .. 0
		50 .. 0 .. 0
15.	Holy Family – Schedone	333 .. 0 .. 0
16.	Holy Family – Raphael	20 .. 0 .. 0
17.	Good Shepherd – Murillo	10 .. 0 .. 0
18.	[illegible] – Teniers	5 .. 0 .. 0
19.	Last Supper – Taddeo Zucchero	6 .. 0 .. 0
20.	Boors at Supper – Teniers	
21.	Christ & St. John – Parmeggiano	100 .. 0 .. 0
22.	Cupid from Correggio by Albano	20 .. 0 .. 0
23.	Cupids – Correggio	35 .. 0 .. 0
24.	Old Portrait – Aldegraf	10 .. 0 .. 0
25. 26.	[illegible] / Bathsheba } – Luca Giordano	10 .. 0 .. 0
27.	Madonna & Child – Old German Master	20 .. 0 .. 0
28.	Two Circular Landscapes – Teniers	40 .. 0 .. 0
29.	Las Gallegas – Murillo	140 .. 0 .. 0
31.	Madonna & Child – A. Caracci	20 .. 0 .. 0
32.	Judith – Bronzini	40 .. 0 .. 0
33.	St. Francis – Albert Durer	8 .. 0 .. 0
34.	Magdalen – Guercino	60 .. 0 .. 0
35.	Parnassus – Cav: Arpino	50 .. 0 .. 0
	all these in Drawing Room –	1487 .. 0 .. 0

Fig. 3. Lord Heytesbury's 1843 inventory of pictures, listing the Philadelphia *Saint Francis*, number 31, as the work of Albrecht Dürer.

Fig. 4. Addendum to Lord Heytesbury's 1843 inventory of pictures giving the cost of the Philadelphia *Saint Francis* as £8. Here the painting is listed as number 33.

that the Heytesbury picture must have been produced in Spain.

This observation concerning the different colors of Franciscan habits (a point that recurs in the literature without resolution) has been considerably muddled. There was no set canon in the fifteenth century for the color of Franciscan robes. The saint himself is shown variously in a black, gray, or brown habit, as are other friars. The color distinction for Franciscans arises only in the sixteenth century with the establishment of the Order of Friars Minor Capuchin.

Sir William Martin Conway took up Weale's observation in 1887, stating that some scholars believed the English picture to be a copy of the one in Turin.[13] In 1888 Henri Hymans elaborated on the argument, stating that Waagen's speculation on a Portuguese origin should be dismissed on the basis of the Adornes document, which indicated the presence of the pictures back in Bruges by 1470. Hymans illustrated two drawings of kneeling donors, which he took to be models for the wings that the testament stipulated be added to both of the Saint Francis "portraits" (fig. 7).[14] No historian seems to have taken up Hymans's connection of these portraits with the wings requested in the will. Whatever their purpose, the drawings appear stylistically to date from the early sixteenth century (or, more likely, they are nineteenth-century copies) and relate closely to the beautiful stained-glass portraits of the family in their mortuary chapel, the Jeruzalemkapel, attached to their palace in Bruges, which was dedicated to the Holy Sepulchre in Jerusalem.

The comparison of the Turin and Philadelphia pictures began in earnest in the late nineteenth century, establishing the issue—the precedence of one or the other and their mutual (or independent) relationship to Jan van Eyck, his workshop, and followers—as one of the thorniest conundrums in the study of Early Netherlandish art. An exhibition held in 1983 at the Jeruzalemkapel in Bruges has clarified much about the Adornes family and its economic and cultural connection to Flanders, Burgundy, and beyond.[15] It would be difficult to overstate the importance of the Adornes family in the economy and politics of Flanders. While retaining links to their ancestral city of Genoa, the family had an office in Flanders as early as 1260.

Fig. 5. The Philadelphia
Saint Francis before 1906.

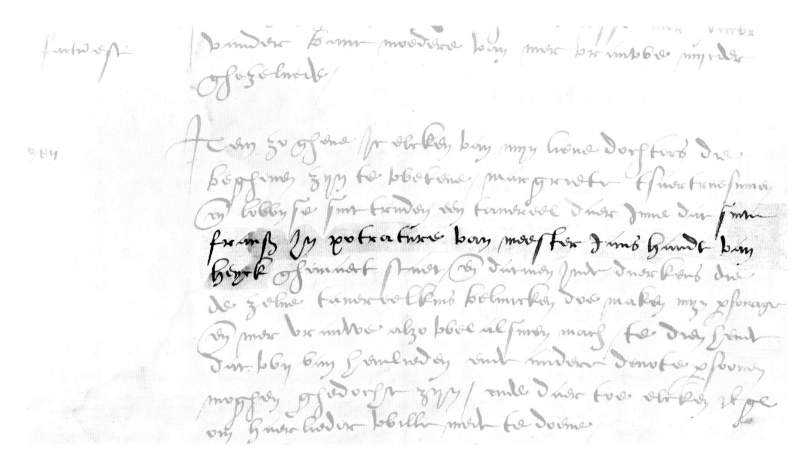

Fig. 6. Sixteenth-century transcription of the will of Anselme Adornes, February 10, 1470 (pl. XIX from C. Aru and E. de Geradon, *La Galerie Sabauda de Turin*, vol. 5 of *Les Primitifs flamands: 1. Corpus de la peinture des anciens Pays-Bas méridionaux au quinzième siècle* [Antwerp, 1952]). The highlighted portion reads, "Saint Francis in portraiture from the hand of Master Jan van Eyck."

Anselme was, among other things, "Seigneur de Covalhui, Gentbrugghe, Jerusalem et de Ste. Catherine du Mont Sinai"; "cavalier du St. Sepulcre, de l'order royal de la Licorne d'Ecosse et de l'ordre dy Sultan de Perse"; "forestier de la Société de l'ourse blanc" in 1444; "chef-homme" in 1450, 1456, 1458, 1460, 1463, and 1473; "Tresoirer" in 1459, 1463, and 1464; Burgermeister of Bruges in 1475; counselor to Charles the Bold and to James III, king of Scotland (where he had an office in connection with the wool trade), and served Philip the Good and Charles the Bold on several diplomatic missions.[16] His father, Pierre, held equal rank and power, and it was he who received a papal bull in 1435 to construct a family chapel dedicated to the Holy Sepulchre in Jerusalem, a project completed by Anselme. Anselme traveled at least twice to the East to visit the Holy Sepulchre in Jerusalem while he was constructing his chapel in Bruges, which would contain a reproduction of Christ's tomb in that most holy of all pilgrimage sites.

I dwell on the biographical details of the Adornes family for several reasons. It is often overlooked that Anselme survived his trip to the East that had prompted the 1470 testament, living on to meet a terrible death thirteen years later (he was assassinated at Linlithgow, near Edinburgh, leaving a sapphire ring to the bishop of that city). There is no evidence that either of his daughters ever received her legacy, despite historians' efforts to trace both pictures through them. At the time of her father's pilgrimage, Marguerite, born in 1448, was in the Carthusian nunnery near Bruges, Sint-Anna ter Woestijne. Precise documentation of her death date does not survive. Louise, born in 1457, was a regular canoness in the abbey of Sint-Truiden as late as 1493.[17] Of particular significance in regard to the two paintings of Saint Francis is the family's connection to the Franciscan order, which has been overlooked in the Van Eyck literature.

As has often been observed, representations of Saint Francis are rare in Northern Europe in the fifteenth century. While the order was extremely active[18]—its quarters in Bruges now house the Groeningemuseum—few, if any, works are known to have been direct commissions. Saint Francis appears, albeit with many other saints, in one of three opulent copes (now in the Kunsthistorisches Museum, Vienna) made for the Order of the Golden Fleece and thought to have been produced in Bruges around 1430 (fig. 8). Other early representations of the stigmatization occur north of the Alps in the Book of Hours of the Marechal de Boucicaut (Musée Jacquemart-André, Paris), in

Fig. 7. Kneeling donors, reproduced in Henri Hymans, "Le Saint François d'Assise de Jean van Eyck," *Gazette des Beaux-Arts*, 2nd period, vol. 37 (1888), pp. 78–79.

the Beaufort Psalter (British Museum, London), and in the so-called Hours of Mary of Saint Pol (Cambridge University, Dd. 5.5f 338v).[19] While these suggest the ongoing power of this image throughout Europe, none bears any direct relationship to the Philadelphia and Turin pictures. The Franciscans, however, were entrusted with the care of the Holy Sepulchre in Jerusalem. Given the Adornes family's devotion to that holy shrine (documented in 1435, six years before the death of Van Eyck, during the life of Pierre Adornes, by the papal bull concerning a family chapel dedicated to the Holy Sepulchre), the cult of the Holy Sepulchre and its connection with the Franciscan order in Bruges remains a fertile area of investigation. Anselme also requested that his pallbearers be Franciscan friars in his testament that mentions the two images of Saint Francis.

The Adornes held a position in the Burgun-dian court and the economy of Bruges equal to, if not higher than, the Arnolfinis, at the time of Van Eyck's activity in that city. It is possible that Pierre commissioned both paintings of Saint Francis; Anselme, as the oldest son, would have inherited his father's most prized possessions. As circumstantial as such speculation may be, it clearly merits further study.

Another light that can be thrown on the early history of the pictures is the existence of two additional paintings that clearly reflect knowledge of the Eyckian Saint Francis composition. One is a rather beautiful picture now in the Prado (fig. 9). Documentation places this work in the Royal Collection at La Granja in 1746, where it was inventoried as by Joachim Patinir.[20] Max Friedländer attributed the painting to the Master of Hoogstraeten; the city in the background has been identified as Dinant.[21] The vertical format of this composition suggests

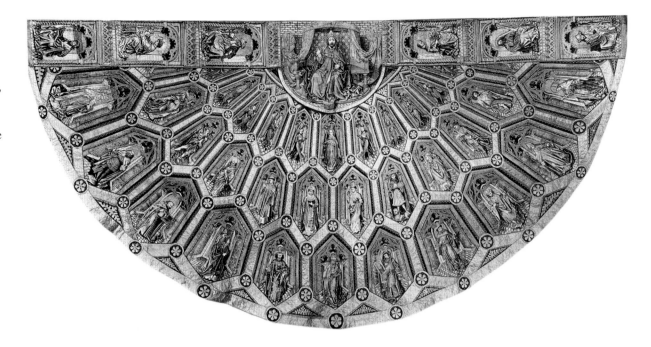

Fig. 8. Ordination cope of the Order of the Golden Fleece, possibly designed by Jan van Eyck, c. 1430, Kunsthistorisches Museum, Vienna, inv. no. 19.

Detail of fig. 8 showing the figure of Saint Francis on the ordination cope of the Order of the Golden Fleece.

that it may reflect the Philadelphia picture with its later addition still attached (fig. 5). Remnants of that addition, which was removed by Roger Fry in 1906, now form the top border of the Johnson picture and show considerable age.[22] The problematic upturned foot of Brother Leo, which, for many historians, indicated that the Turin version was a misunderstood copy of the Johnson picture (until the position of the foot was revealed to be a clumsy restoration), is eliminated in the Prado picture. The mute passivity of Saint Francis, which, for Erwin Panofsky, called both pictures into doubt as lacking the expressive subtlety of Jan van Eyck,[23] has been "corrected." In the Prado picture, Francis gazes up directly at the vision of the cross. Also, the alleged awkwardness of Saint Francis's position—the placement of the knees, the turn of his bare feet—has been made rational.

The other visual record of the continued presence of one or the other of the primary images in the North is a more passive and banal copy, produced perhaps in Brussels around 1500 (fig. 10).[24] It was last recorded in 1928 in an Amsterdam sale of the collection of Amédée Prouvost of Roubaix. Its scale—12⅛ by 15¾ inches—suggests that it is a fairly literal, if generalized, copy after the Turin picture. While it is difficult to judge details from the extant photograph, the misunderstood foot of Brother Leo suggests that the awkward restoration of the Turin picture, which brought about this mistake, happened quite early in the life of the picture.

Sparse concrete evidence to support so many

words written in the literature about the Philadelphia and Turin pictures, certainly. Yet Otto Pächt's summation of the state of scholarship concerning the Van Eyck literature as "unedifying" is,[25] perhaps, too harsh, even if Panofsky knew exactly the power of his opinion when he noted his dismissal of both pictures from the Van Eyck canon as "heresy."[26] The problem is further complicated by the recent restoration of the Turin picture, which reveals it as a work of extreme refinement and depth of feeling.

My own view is that the Philadelphia *Saint*

Fig. 9. Attributed to the Master of Hoogstraeten (Netherlandish, active c. 1485–c. 1520), *The Stigmatization of Saint Francis*, panel, 18½ x 13¾" (47 x 35 cm), Museo del Prado, Madrid, inv. no. 1617.

Fig. 10. Copy after Jan van Eyck, *The Stigmatization of Saint Francis*, c. 1500, 12⅛ x 15¾" (30.8 x 40 cm), last recorded in 1928 at an Amsterdam sale of the collection of Amédée Prouvost of Roubaix.

Francis—very like its sister in Turin—is an object of remarkable intensity and profound piety. I find that those things Panofsky thought to be feeble—the abstract passivity of Saint Francis, the unnaturalness of his anatomy—can be viewed just as readily as positive qualities. The isolated containment of Francis, his resigned acceptance of his miraculous bodily torment, elevate him to a figure of saintly piety, in a manner far exceeding the requirements of mundane narrative. The unnatural position of his feet, often observed as an anatomical anomaly, is crucial to our understanding of the miracle of the stigmatization: both fresh wounds are thus visible on the soles of his feet. To accomplish the torque of the figure, the artist has necessarily blurred the exact placement of the knees underneath the beautiful pour of drapery that firmly grounds Francis in the field of flowers and leaves no doubt of his bodily substance amid the unworldly clarity of light and space enveloping him. Leo is his Sancho Panza, more literally described, almost to the point of comic tenderness.

Such subjective views are, of course, what drive our concern about pictures and lead to the fervor of diverse opinions that makes these paintings, and our understanding of them, so richly perplexing. The essays that follow will maintain sterner and more objective standards and will support the position that this problem is hardly at a standstill, despite the continuing number of standoffs. If anything, the essays demonstrate the immense amount of new directions and information to explore.

1. Frank Jewett Mather, Jr., "Recent Additions to the Collection of Mr. John G. Johnson, Philadelphia," *The Burlington Magazine*, vol. 9 (1906), pp. 358–59; C. Ricketts, "Pictures in the Collection of Mr. John G. Johnson, of Philadelphia," *The Burlington Magazine*, vol. 9 (1906), p. 426.

2. *Dictionary of National Biography*, ed. Sir Leslie Stephen and Sir Sidney Lee (Oxford, 1959–60), vol. 9, p. 779, s.v. "Heytesbury."

3. In 1955 transcriptions of the correspondence concerning the shipment of works were generously provided by Baron Heytesbury in correspondence with Barbara Sweeny, then curator of the Johnson Collection. Curatorial files, Department of European Painting, Philadelphia Museum of Art.

4. Photocopies of this inventory as well as transcriptions of the correspondence mentioned above were provided by Baron Heytesbury. The Philadelphia *Saint Francis* appears in two separate inventories of paintings owned by the first Lord Heytesbury, one of which records value and the other, the location of paintings within his house. On both lists, drawn up in 1843, the painting is described and attributed to Albrecht Dürer, not Jan van Eyck. However, the two lists are numbered differently: the painting is listed as item 33 in the inventory that details prices paid by Lord Heytesbury, and number 31 in the list that describes their placement in his house. Photographs of these two inventories are in the curatorial files, Department of European Painting, Philadelphia Museum of Art.

5. G. F. Waagen, *Galleries and Cabinets of Art in Great Britain. . .*, vol. 4 (supplement) of *Treasures of Art in Great Britain, 1854–1857* (London, 1857), p. 389.

6. British Institution, London, 1865, no. 41; Royal Academy, London, 1886, no. 198 (as 8 x 6½"). See Algernon Graves, *A Century of Loan Exhibitions, 1813–1912* (London, 1914), vol. 4, pp. 1537–38. Claude Phillips doubted the attribution to Van Eyck in "Correspondance d'Angleterre: Expositions d'hiver de la Royal Academy et de la Grosvenor Gallery à Londres," *La Chronique des Arts et de la Curiosité* (1886), p. 15.

7. Henri Hymans, "Le Saint François d'Assise de Jean van Eyck," *Gazette des Beaux-Arts*, 2nd period, vol. 37 (1888), pp. 78–83.

8. Roger Fry published a letter in the May 1926 *Burlington Magazine* (of which he was founder and editor) describing his treatment of the Philadelphia *Saint Francis* for John G. Johnson some twenty years earlier. He described his reaction to this picture (he was certain it was a work by Hubert van Eyck and that the Turin painting was a copy), the state of the picture, and the actions he took to rectify it. Fry described the panel's state and his measurements as follows: "Mr. Johnson handed it to me to clean whilst I was in new York. . . . When it came to me, the panel was considerably larger at the top, and a dull, opaque sky concealed the join where the extra piece had been added on to satisfy some owner who did not appreciate the compressed composition of the original. The sky had been enlivened, if I remember right, with a crowd of small white, cloud-like forms suggesting the presence of a cohort of angels. These all came away with the sky and then, to my surprise, I found that the original panel appeared surrounded by a brilliant scarlet margin, painted on the panel, just as might have been seen on the border of a manuscript illumination. I suppose this is now covered by the frame, as the photograph shows no trace of it. This border made me suppose that van Eyck had conceived this as a miniature in oil on panel, and that it might indicate a date not very far removed from the drawings of the Turin *Book of Hours*. Brother Leo's head was completely repainted, but the repainting came away, though not so easily as the false sky had done, and revealed the original in almost perfect condition. Altogether, the repaintings appear to have been entirely gratuitous and undertaken with a view to 'improving' the picture" (Editorial Letter, *The Burlington Magazine*, vol. 48 [1926], p. 274). Many of Fry's memories about the painting are validated by the archival photograph (fig. 5) of the painting taken before his 1906 treatment. Sadly, none of Fry's notes from the time of the actual cleaning or photographic documentation of his work appear to have survived.

9. Alexandre Pinchart, ed., *Archives des arts, sciences et lettres: Documents inédits* (Ghent, 1860), vol. 1, p. 267.

10. "Item zo gheve ic elcken van myne lieve dochters die begheven zyn, te wetene Margriete, tSaertreusinnen, ende Lowyse Sint Truden, een tavereel daerinne dat sinte Franciscus in potrature van meester Jans handt van Heyck ghemaect staet, ende dat men in de duerkens die van de zelve tavereelkins beluicken, doe maken myn personage ender mer vrauwe, also wel als men mach. . . ." Testament of Anselme Adornes, February 10, 1470, transcription, Stadsarchief, Bruges (no. 1, article 22). Text collated by Philips Cools, notary public, and published by A. De Poorter, "Testament van Anselmus Adornes, 10 Febr. 1470," *Biekorf* (Bruges), vol. 37 (1931), pp. 225–39. Transcription from C. Aru and E. de Geradon, *La Galerie Sabauda de Turin*, vol. 5 of *Les Primitifs flamands: 1. Corpus de la peinture des anciens Pays-Bas méridionaux au quinzième siècle* (Antwerp, 1952), p. 13. In 1953 Erwin Panofsky (*Early Netherlandish Painting: Its Origins and Character* [Cambridge, Mass., 1953], vol. 1, p. 192, n. 1) noted that the Adornes will was a sixteenth-century copy and pointed out the awkwardness of the language describing the two paintings. He suggested that an interpolation had been committed by the sixteenth-century scribe and suggested several interpretations for the meaning of the focal sentence, but doubted that the paintings mentioned in the will referred to the Philadelphia and Turin paintings. Jan van der Stock noted that this translation does not reflect the awkward inversion of word order in the will, which reads, literally, as from the "Master Jan hand Van Eyck." Unfortunately, the sixteenth-century copy of the Adornes will cannot be found in the Bruges Stadsarchief.

11. W. H. James Weale, "John van Eyck at the Academy Old Masters Exhibition," *The Times* (London), February 3, 1886, p. 7.

12. Anselme Adornes would have been seventeen, not fifteen, years old in 1441, when Van Eyck died.

13. William Martin Conway, *Early Flemish Artists and Their Predecessors on the Lower Rhine* (London, 1887), p. 141, n. 1.

14. Hymans, 1888, pp. 78–83.

15. See A. Vandewalle, *Adornes en Jeruzalem: International levens in het 15de- en 16de-eeuwse Brugge*, Bruges, September 9–25, 1983. Further information about Adornes

family documents was kindly supplied by Noël Geirnart, archivist at the Bruges Stadsarchief, in correspondence with Marigene Butler in 1988. Curatorial files, Department of European Paintings, Philadelphia Museum of Art. See also Maximiliaan P. J. Martens, "New Information on Petrus Christus's Biography and the Patronage of His Brussels *Lamentation*," *Simiolus*, vol. 20, no. 1 (1990/91), p. 14 n. 62.

16. See Jean-Jacques Gailliard, *Bruges et le Franc: ou, Leur magistrature et leur nobless avec des données historiques et généalogique sur chaque famille* (Bruges, 1857), vol. 3, p. 103.

17. Noël Geirnart kindly shared this information with Marigene Butler in his 1988 correspondence. Curatorial files, Department of European Painting, Philadelphia Museum of Art.

18. For an introduction to the Franciscan orders in the North see John R. H. Moorman, *A History of the Franciscan Order from Its Origins Until the Year 1517* (Oxford, 1968); and Moorman, *Medieval Franciscan Houses* (New York, 1983). The latter (p. 91), gives a brief survey of the documentation of the order in Bruges, first founded in 1221 and moved within the walls of the city in 1233. The new church was "built by merchants, some of them Florentine."

19. Judith Stein researched the occurrence of early representations of Saint Francis in Northern Europe in an unpublished paper written at the University of Pennsylvania in 1974. Copy, curatorial files, Department of European Painting, Philadelphia Museum of Art.

20. Don Pedro de Madrazo, director of the Prado, attributed this painting to Joachim Patinir and suggested that the figures had been painted by Albrecht Dürer, in his *Catálogo de los cuadros del Museo Nacional de Pintura y escultura* (Madrid, 1876). The presence of the painting at La Granja by 1746 was noted in the 1949 *Museo del Prado, Catálogo* (Madrid, 1949), p. 195, with an introduction by F. J. Sanchez Canton.

21. Friedländer's attribution is reported in the 1949 *Museo del Prado, Catálogo* (Madrid, 1949), p. 195, which also identified the city as Dinant.

22. This observation could lead to speculation that the addition was put on the Johnson version to accommodate vertical donor wings (such as were illustrated by Hymans, 1888, pp. 78–79 [fig. 7]), but this argument is, perhaps, empty. Marigene Butler believes that the remnants of the addition on the top border of the picture predates the nineteenth century and that the format of the picture was altered at an earlier date.

23. Panofsky, 1953, vol. 1, p. 192, n.1.

24. See Albert Heyse, "Un primitif flamand de la collection de Mr. Amédée Prouvost de Roubaix," *Gand Artistique*, vol. 5 (1926), pp. 222–23. Heyse calls the picture "essentiellement flamande"; the attribution here is the author's.

25. Otto Pächt, "The Literature of Art: A New Book on the Van Eycks," *The Burlington Magazine*, vol. 95 (1953), p. 253.

26. Panofsky, 1953, vol. 1, p. 192, n.1.

Carlenrica Spantigati

The Turin Van Eyck "Saint Francis Receiving the Stigmata"

Among the many problems that modern critics writing about Jan van Eyck periodically face, often with divergent conjectures and conclusions, is the one raised by the existence of two small paintings representing Saint Francis of Assisi Receiving the Stigmata, one in the John G. Johnson Collection at the Philadelphia Museum of Art (pl. I), the other in the Galleria Sabauda in Turin (pl. II, fig. 11).[1]

That both works belong to the Van Eyck circle is indisputable, but are they both by the master's hand? Or, is one—and which one—a slightly later copy of the other, which would then constitute a single authentic work? Or, do both derive from a lost original?

The differences between these hypotheses are considerable, and seem not to allow for definitive interpretations; but at this time, as a result of recent, detailed analyses of both paintings on the occasions of their respective restorations, it is possible to bring the problem into better focus. Indeed, the collaboration between the Philadelphia Museum of Art and the Galleria Sabauda in Turin, which has taken concrete form in the joint presentation of studies on the two works, offers significant and useful points of departure for scholarly investigation.

The present essay will be confined to the Turin painting, which was intelligently restored in 1982 at the skillful hands of Guido and Anna Rosa Nicola in Aramengo, in the province of Asti.[2]

Consideration of the intricate problem of attribution raised by the "twin" paintings has always referred to the will drawn up in Bruges on February 10, 1470, by Anselme Adornes (1424–1483). From the important Genoese family of the Adornos, Anselme belonged to a branch that had been transplanted to Flanders. An important figure at the court of Burgundy, he drafted the testament on the eve of a long and arduous journey that was to take him through Italy and to the Holy Land on official business for the duke Charles the Bold.[3]

Despite reservations about the document, known only from a sixteenth-century transcription (fig. 6),[4] one naturally focuses on the paragraph in which Adornes declares that he bequeaths to each of two of his daughters, Marguerite and Louise, at Carthusian convents near Bruges and at Sint-Truiden,[5] a picture representing "sinte Franciscus in potrature van meester Jans handt van Heyck" (Saint Francis in portraiture from the hand of Master Jan van Eyck). The

Fig. 11. The Galleria
Sabauda, Turin *Saint
Francis Receiving the
Stigmata* after 1982 treat-
ment. 11½ x 13⅛"
(29.2 x 33.4 cm).

bequest also includes an order to have portraits of Anselme Adornes and his wife, Marguerite van der Bank, painted with great care on side panels.[6]

The will dates from February 1470, but Anselme Adornes was not to die until some years later, on January 23, 1483. His was a violent death, following a series of vicissitudes that had taken him to the court of James III, king of Scotland. About a month before his death, on December 7, 1482, he had drawn up a new will that did not, however, mention the "little pictures."[7]

The enigma of the two pictures may be approached from the point of view of their histories. What are the provenances of the Philadelphia and Turin versions of *Saint Francis Receiving the Stigmata*? Henri Hymans, who in 1883 attributed the Turin work to Jan van Eyck, reported what he had learned firsthand from Francesco Gamba, director of the Galleria Sabauda from 1869.[8] The same information is subsequently reported by Max Friedländer and, with slight variation, by Carlo Aru.[9] Let us follow what is stated by Hymans, whose sources are certainly reliable not only because the incumbent director of the Turin museum informed him directly, but because of the ability and seriousness with which Gamba did his job.[10]

The work was acquired in 1866, when Massimo D'Azeglio, then director of the Turin museum, bought the small painting vaguely identified as being of the "Flemish School" from Luigi Fascio, mayor of Feletto Canavese, in the province of Turin. The latter, in turn, had acquired it from Professor Bonzani of Casale Monferrato, in the province of Alessandria, who had come into possession of it from an "ex-nun" also living in Casale.

At this point the provenance abruptly breaks off. It is indeed a curious coincidence that the painting was in the possession of a nun, assuming it could have been the same one bequeathed by Anselme Adornes to a cloistered daughter three and a half centuries earlier. In addition, the presence in Piedmont of several important families with documented contacts with Flanders has been noted. For example, the Villa family of Chieri commissioned a triptych from Rogier van der Weyden.[11] The Genoese branch of the Adorno family, moreover, held lands in the Alessandria area, in a strip of territory that at the time did not form part of Monferrato but was politically dependent on Genoa.[12]

The references to ownership by the "ex-nun" vaguely date to the beginning of the nineteenth century, in the stormy years following Napoleon's suppression of ecclesiastical orders, resulting in the dispersal and loss of the furnishings of many convents.[13] As for Casale Monferrato itself, the journal kept by the canon Giuseppe de Conti provides a dramatic picture of these events.[14] The congregations of nuns dissolved at that time in Casale Monferrato were those of the Dominican Sisters of the church of Santa Caterina, the Poor Clares of the church of Santa Maria Maddalena, the Capuchin Sisters of Santa Chiara, the Augustinian Sisters of San Bartolomeo, the Virgins of Saint Ursula, and the Tertiary Dominican Lay Sisters of the Blessed Margherita of Savoy.[15]

But there are still far too many missing pieces to hope for a tidy solution to the puzzle. The nun's name is not known to us, nor is the order to which she belonged. One might also surmise that the painting *Saint Francis Receiving the Stigmata* was an object of private and personal devotion and did not constitute part of the official property of her convent.

Nor are the documents relating to the Galleria Sabauda and kept at the Soprintendenza per i Beni Artistici e Storici in Turin (which oversees the museum) of much help. Aru has noted that sections of the archives were lost during World War II.[16] At the bottom of the nineteenth-century file known as the Vico holdings[17] is a reply sent on June 26, 1863, by Massimo D'Azeglio to Luigi Gandolfi, then inspector at the Galleria Sabauda, concerning the purchase of an otherwise unspecified "Flemish" painting that Gandolfi proposed purchasing. The judgment of the director of the Galleria was favorable, but he rejected the proposal on other grounds having to do with the programs then in progress: "having, that is, to complete the Piedmontese School, and after that, save up for the purchase of one of the important items that we lack. If exceptions were to be made at every moment, our capital would be frittered away.... Therefore the price of the proposed painting being [so much] higher, and since we are already rich in Flemish works, I think it better that we keep to our purpose."[18]

It would be interesting to know what painting was being offered, its subject, and its period, though it is doubtful that it could have been the Van Eyck, which was purchased three years later. All the more reason why one would like to know the details of the purchase contract for *Saint Francis Receiving the Stigmata* and why it was deemed unnecessary to adhere to the 1863 stricture of singular purpose in acquisition, a declaration primarily expressed by people well aware of the importance of the "Maestri oltremontani," which were richly represented in the Galleria.[19] It seems likely that the Van Eyck entered the museum's collections quietly: the *Indicazione sommaria dei quadri e capi d'arte della R. Pinacoteca di Torino*, prepared by Giovanni Vico and published in Florence in 1866, places it in Room XII: "no. 313, Flemish School, Saint Francis and a friar." The same identification appears in the edition reprinted in Turin in 1881; however, the revised edition of the *Guida ad indicazione sommaria*, prepared by Gamba in 1883, records with alacrity Hymans's attribution to Jan van Eyck and the correct description of the subject.[20]

As unfortunately sometimes happens, the research conducted so far has not come up with anything effectual for unraveling the tangled skein. All that can be done is to reexamine the painting analytically in search of whatever information it alone can supply.

First of all, one might point out the fundamental element that strips away any confused or contradictory interpretations concerning the attribution: the quality of the work's execution. Now that, in the course of restoration, cleaning has removed the (modern) yellowed varnish and some repainting in the landscape and figures (fig. 12),[21] the quality emerges as especially high. The composition is carefully gauged in its presentation of the friars in the foreground and the backdrop of rocks on the right, which opens onto the receding, well-defined landscape shimmering in the distance (figs. 13, 14). The crystalline light, which owes much to the technique of execution, achieves extraordinary effects of transparency in the city in the background, in the pale blue mountain chain lost in the distance, and in the rocks, trees, flowers, and clouds, across which a flight of birds passes. Once again, it is possible to perceive the transparency of the water gushing from the rocks at Brother Leo's feet in the foreground and the touches of light that form the knots and tassels on the cords of the robes of the two friars (fig. 15). Nor is it perhaps even necessary to call

Fig. 12. Detail of the Turin *Saint Francis*, partially cleaned.

attention to the delicate execution of Saint Francis's face, carefully defined on the forehead plane, furrowed by slight but numerous wrinkles, the expressive eyes, and the composition of mouth, chin, and cheeks, on which a slight growth of beard is apparent (fig. 16).

Another element is decisive: the "illuminated-manuscript" quality of certain features of the painting, such as the tiny, lively figures that populate the road and wood behind Saint Francis or those enlivening the stretch of land before the walls of the city. To call attention to the qualities in the *Saint Francis Receiving the Stigmata* that resemble illuminations raises another important problem concerning Jan van Eyck. I do not intend to go into the knotty, critical question of the miniatures of the Turin-Milan Hours,[22] but Jan's name is connected with this undertaking. On the other hand, it is just such

Fig. 13. Detail of Brother
Leo from the Turin *Saint
Francis*.

Fig. 14. Detail of the
Turin *Saint Francis*.

Fig. 15. Detail of the foreground with Brother Leo's feet from the Turin *Saint Francis*.

Fig. 16. Detail of the Turin *Saint Francis*.

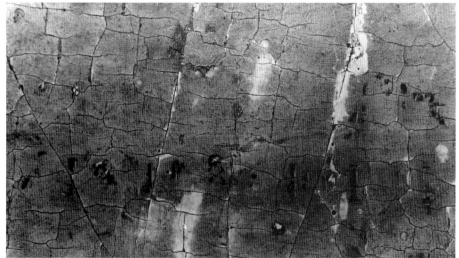

Fig. 17. Marbleized reverse of the Turin *Saint Francis*.

Fig. 18. Obliterated inscription on the rock to the right of the seraph-Christ in the Turin *Saint Francis*.

small-scale paintings attributable to him with certainty that confirm his undoubted talents and propensities for producing works of miniature dimensions.[23]

The authenticity of the Turin painting is clearly supported by the technical and visual comparisons proposed by Charles Sterling between it and the *Virgin of Chancellor Rolin* (fig. 105), particularly the landscape with the detail of the boat and its shadow reflected in the water (fig. 14), and the use of a marbleized reddish brown color spread on the back of both panels (fig. 17).[24]

Visual elements, the quality of the technical execution, and, in particular, the range of color in relation to its luminosity all attest to the work's authenticity. And more information has

been added by the reflectographic examination carried out on the Turin work by J.R.J. van Asperen de Boer, at the request of the Philadelphia Museum of Art.[25]

Unfortunately, restoration could do no more than indicate the former existence of an inscription on the rock to the immediate right of the seraph-Christ, an inscription irremediably obliterated in the past that cannot be reconstructed (fig. 18).[26]

The iconographic curiosity of the brown-colored cowl of Saint Francis has been much remarked upon.[27] The brown habit of the Reformed Franciscans was known in the Low Countries only toward the end of the fifteenth century, well after Van Eyck's death, but had appeared throughout southern Europe by the time the *Saint Francis* was painted.[28]

Another important and often-noted iconographic element is the preponderance of specific flora, as in certain panels of the Ghent altarpiece (fig. 19). In the past these elements were seen as being connected with Van Eyck's documented travels in Spain and Portugal in 1428–29.[29] One might add the more general observation that the overall iconography of Saint Francis Receiving the Stigmata was common at the time in the Mediterranean area, but rarely to be found in northern Europe.[30]

But Sterling further noted in this painting— as in the *Virgin of Chancellor Rolin* (fig. 105), the *Three Marys at the Sepulchre* in Rotterdam (fig. 20), the *Crucifixion* in New York (fig. 21), and the panel with the Soldiers of Christ in the Ghent altarpiece—the presence of snow-covered mountain chains, a motif that could be the result of the artist having seen the Alps or the Pyrenees.[31] And yet, his journeys to Spain and Portugal were surely made by sea. How then, and when, should we place this direct visual evidence of exposure to Alpine ranges?

Sterling pointed out in the landscapes of certain paintings the presence of buildings that can clearly be identified with monuments in Jerusalem (for example, the Mosque of Omar), and, in comparing these correspondences with documented reports of payments to Van Eyck by the treasury of the duke of Burgundy for a journey in 1426 that was deliberately kept secret, he deduced that in that year the artist had been sent on a mission to the Holy Land. He speculated that Van Eyck would have made this journey to Palestine by way of Italy, with

Fig. 19. Detail of flora in
the Ghent altarpiece, St.
Bavo's Cathedral, Ghent.

Fig. 20. Circle of Jan van
Eyck, *The Three Marys at
the Sepulchre*, panel,
28⅛ x 35" (71.5 x 89 cm),
Museum Boymans–van
Beuningen, Rotterdam,
inv. no. 2449.

Fig. 21. Jan van Eyck,
The Crucifixion, canvas,
transferred from panel,
22¼ x 7¾" (56.5 x 19.7 cm),
The Metropolitan
Museum of Art, New York,
Fletcher Fund, 33.92a.

Fig. 22. Detail of the cityscape in the Turin *Saint Francis*.

certain plausible stops. Thus, it would even be justifiable to identify the appearance of the rocks on the right of the *Saint Francis* with the real landscape of La Verna, the site of the saint's miracle.[32]

Sterling advanced a few cautious hypotheses about the commission of the painting,[33] which was known in Florence in the 1470s: E. H. Gombrich has pointed out the connections between certain of Leonardo's drawings dating from around 1473 and the landscapes in the *Saint Francis* and the Ghent altarpiece.[34] But as Günter Panhans has clearly shown,[35] there is even more convincing proof of the Florentine fame of the *Saint Francis*: the city in the background (fig. 22) is repeated with absolute precision in the *Adoration of the Magi* attributed to Botticelli, dated between 1470 and 1475, and now in the National Gallery, London (fig. 104).[36]

The fact that Flemish painting enjoyed a certain popularity in Florence is nothing new

and can in any case be discerned throughout the century, but why was it not until the 1470s that the landscape of the *Saint Francis* was repeated in Florence?[37] Sterling's cautious hypothesis that, early on, the painting was present in Italy would not fully answer the question. And, if the work is really the one mentioned in Anselme Adornes's will, then it was surely in Bruges in February 1470.

Immediately after drawing up the often-cited will, Anselme Adornes left on the official mission entrusted to him by Charles the Bold, the journey to the Holy Land that would keep him far from Bruges until August 1471. He was accompanied by high officials of the Burgundian court, and their most important stops along the way are known: on March 20 he was in Milan, later in Genoa, and finally in Rome, where he was received twice by Pope Paul II. His journey to Palestine completed, he returned to Italy—stopping in Naples on December 21, in Rome in

Fig. 23. Detail of the Turin *Saint Francis*.

Fig. 24. Jan van Eyck, *Portrait of Cardinal Albergati*, silverpoint, 8⅜ x 7⅛" (21.4 x 18.1 cm), Kunsthistorisches Museum, Dresden, inv. no. c775.

January, and then in Florence—and, proceeding northward by way of the Tyrol, he arrived back in Bruges on August 14.[38] At every stage of this important journey Anselme was warmly received at the various Italian courts, both as the representative of the duke of Burgundy and as an eminent member of the Adorno family. If the painting *Saint Francis Receiving the Stigmata* had been, at one time, connected with the artist's official, albeit secret, mission to Palestine in 1426, its modest dimensions certainly would not have prevented its owner from carrying it with him in 1470 as a picture for private devotions and showing it to his distinguished hosts during his brief stops in Italy.

When should one place the date of execution of the Turin painting? Most art historians are inclined to date it around the middle of the 1430s, but Sterling put it slightly earlier, around 1432.[39] If the connections, including the visual ones (the Alpine range, the rocks of La Verna), with Van Eyck's mysterious 1426 journey are convincing, the painting could have been developed at a later date. What is required in this vein is a stylistic examination of the panel and a comparison with other undisputed works by the master, which, however, all date from between 1432 and 1441. On that basis, the particular use of light developed by Jan van Eyck and his way of creating the folds of draperies allow one to place the work at the beginning of the 1430s.

The face of Saint Francis, as has been noted, has all the marks of a portrait (fig. 23).[40] In its subtle definition of planes, and the play of light and color, it is stylistically quite close to the well-known *Portrait of Cardinal Albergati* (Kunsthistorisches Museum, Vienna)—or better still, to its preparatory drawing in Dresden (fig. 24)[41]—and also to that of Chancellor Rolin in the *Virgin of Chancellor Rolin* (fig. 105). Indeed, with the last there is more than one similar external element, such as the hairstyle (especially now that the restoration has removed the repainting that had given Saint Francis a tonsure nonexistent at the time), the line of the mouth, the shape of the ear, so that one is almost tempted to call the Saint Francis a Rolin younger by some five to ten years.

RESTORATION OF THE TURIN PAINTING
Dimensions (panel): 11⅛ x 13⅛" (29.5 x 33.4 cm)
(painted surface): 11½ x 13⅛" (29.2 x 33.4 cm)
Support: Two oak panels (thickness 1.1 cm) joined vertically at the center of the painting; on the back the presence of a band underneath the preparation to protect the joint has been verified. Presumably this band is also present in front. It has not been possible to determine the material of this band (parchment, cloth, or paper).
Ground: Chalk and animal glue.
Reverse: Marbleized, reddish brown paint, worn away in several places (fig. 17). Along the edges at several points, the preparation of

both sides partly covers the thickness of the support.

Inscription: On the large flat mass to the right of the seraph-Christ appear traces of an inscription, scraped away and now illegible (fig. 18).

The painting came to the museum without its original frame.

HISTORY OF MODERN RESTORATIONS
Restoration by E. Patrito, c. 1952[42]

The Nicola Restoration Laboratory, which examined the painting in 1982, has located some of the photographic documentation from this restoration, revealing the prior existence of damage along the edges and of repainting on the tonsure of Saint Francis and in the middle area (Brother Leo's cowl and the vegetation between the two friars).

We must assume that Patrito's operations were confined to fixing the color, lightly cleaning the surface, and reviving the unity of the painting.

The restoration was marked—an extraordinary fact for those days—by a thorough preventive analysis of the painting, with infrared- and ultraviolet-light photographs, macrophotographs, and microchemical examination of a sample area.

In addition, there is considerable documentation of the anatomical details of the figures (mouths, eyes, Saint Francis's ear, hands, feet), side-by-side with the related analysis by ultraviolet filter.

There is also photographic documentation of the inscription on the rocks, which was already obliterated and unable to be reconstructed, along with much documentation of Brother Leo's left foot, which previous restorations (not removed but continued by Patrito) had made anatomically incorrect.

Restoration Laboratory of the Soprintendenza per i Beni Artistici e Storici del Piemonte, restorer Elvio Gamarra, 1970

After minute and extensive cracking of the painted surface and a conspicuous loss of paint in Saint Francis's tonsure occurred (fig. 25), a review of the painting's state of preservation was undertaken in 1970.

Particularly serious were the cracks corresponding to the repainting, which, along with the support stucco, was flaking extensively. There were dangerous cracks in the original

paint along the line of the vertical joint of the two panels.

The paint surface was accordingly fixed, a light cleaning was undertaken without removing the repainting, and the head of Saint Francis and the central area between the two friars were unified pictorially (fig. 26).

Guido and Anna Rosa Nicola Restoration Laboratory in Aramengo (Asti), with the collaboration of Gian Luigi Nicola and Nicola Pisano, 1982

Since the problem of extensive cracking had arisen once again and the painting appeared darkened by the yellowing of modern protective varnishes, as well as dulled by albeit not very extensive repainting, the decision was made to undertake a more radical operation.

The cracks revealed by raking-light photographs were tiny but covered the whole surface of the work and were particularly serious along the joint of the two panels (figs. 27, 28). The surface film of paint was therefore fixed with animal glue, and preventive measures undertaken for the cleaning.

X-radiographs did not furnish much to go on, because of the obstacle raised by the lead present in the painting. Photographs by ultraviolet light, however, showed repainting on the cowls of both friars and on the vegetation between them, as well as the presence of problems in Brother Leo's foot (figs. 29, 30).

It was accordingly decided to proceed with the cleaning and removal of the yellowed varnishes and former restorations. In the course of this cleaning, with butyl acetate, methyl ketone, and bistoury, executed under constant control

Fig. 26. Detail of the area between the two friars during the 1970 restoration of the Turin *Saint Francis*.

Fig. 27. Raking-light photograph during the 1982 restoration of the Turin *Saint Francis*.

Fig. 28. Raking-light photograph of the joint of the two panels during the 1982 restoration of the Turin *Saint Francis*.

Fig. 29. Ultraviolet-light photograph during the 1982 restoration of the Turin *Saint Francis*.

Fig. 30. Ultraviolet-light photograph during the 1982 restoration of the Turin *Saint Francis*.

Fig. 31. Detail of birds of prey in the Turin *Saint Francis*.

by ultraviolet light, the presence of repainting emerged in the landscape at the extreme upper left and especially on the tonsure of Saint Francis, which had had the deliberate result, at an undetermined time, of completely altering the original hairstyle.

The cleaning has thus permitted the recovery of the extraordinary original sharpness of color, especially in the landscape background, where the blues and whites of the mountains and the clouds have reemerged, as well as hitherto illegible details, such as the birds of prey perched on the rocky summits above the head of Saint Francis (fig. 31).

The cleaning has likewise made it possible to establish in more correct terms the critical debate about Saint Francis's tonsure and the position of the foot of Brother Leo, now revealed to be the figure's left one, folded under the other crossed leg and exposing the sole.

The next step was a second and final fixing, followed by the pictorial integration of large lacunae, executed by light, dotted application of a watercolor undertone, then varnish paints with essence of turpentine.

Given the dimensions of the painting, it was necessary finally to dot lightly the tiny scalings resulting from the widening of the broad web of cracks.

The back was consolidated and cleaned. Slight traces of the glue used to apply the protective paper border, visible in the photographs published by Aru in 1952, could still be noted.

Both sides were protected by varnish with a base of synthetic retouching resin.

The photographs of the Patrito restoration are in the photographic archive of the Nicola Laboratory in Aramengo. All the other photographs are in the photographic archive of the Soprintendenza per i Beni Artistici e Storici del Piemonte.

In connection with the present study, a special series of photographs was taken by the photographer Riccardo Gonella of Turin.

NOTES

1. See Max J. Friedländer, *Die Van Eyck—Petrus Christus*, vol. 1 of *Die altniederländische Malerei* (Berlin, 1924), pp. 101–2; C. Aru and E. de Geradon, *La Galerie Sabauda de Turin*, vol. 5 of *Les Primitifs flamands: 1. Corpus de la peinture des anciens Pays-Bas méridionaux au quinzième siècle* (Antwerp, 1952), pp. 5–13; Friedländer, *The Van Eycks—Petrus Christus*, vol. 1 of *Early Netherlandish Painting*, trans. Heinz Norden (Leiden and Brussels, 1967), pp. 62–63; Giorgio T. Faggin, *L'opera completa dei van Eyck* (Milan, 1968), no. 5 (with negative opinion on the authenticity of the Turin painting); and Charles Sterling, "Jan van Eyck avant 1432," *Revue de l'Art*, no. 33 (1976), pp. 7–81, esp. pp. 29–30, 53–57.

2. The 1982 restoration was carried out with funds from the Ministry for Cultural and Environmental Resources. See Carlenrica Spantigati, *Pittura fiamminga ed olandese in Galleria Sabauda: Il Principe Eugenio di Savoia-Soissons uomo d'armi e collezionista* (Turin, 1982); and R. Tardito Amerio, *La Galleria Sabauda* (Turin, 1984), pp. 31–43, 76–84.

3. For Anselme Adornes, see J. de Saint-Genois, *Biographie nationale de Belgique* (Brussels, 1866), vol. 1, pp. 73–79; and *Dizionario biografico degli italiani* (Rome, 1960), vol. 1, s.v. "Adorno." The report of the journey to Palestine has been published in *Itinéraire d'Anselme Adorno en Terre Sainte (1470–71)*, ed. and trans. Jacques Heers and Georgette de Groer (Paris, 1978); and Georgette de Groer, "Notes de voyage d'un pèlerin flamand en Italie au XV siècle," in *Objets d'art, collections: Hommage à Hubert Landais* (Paris, 1987), pp. 75–83. Pompeo Litta (*Famiglie celebri d'Italia* [Milan, 1818], vol. 1) indicated that the Bruges branch of the Adorno family (also known as Adornes) died out in 1509.

4. Aru and de Geradon, 1952, p. 13. The perplexities have been summed up by Maria Grazia Paolini ("Problemi antonelliani: I rapporti con la pittura fiamminga," *Storia dell'arte*, nos. 38–40 [1980], pp. 151–66), from whose attributions of the Philadelphia and Turin paintings (as by Petrus Christus after an Eyckian original and a copy by Antonello da Messina, respectively) I heartily dissent.

5. Litta (1818) names the two daughters in question as Margherita, described as a Carthusian nun in Bruges, and Caterina, a Celestine nun in Ghent. Anselme Adornes had twelve children, including, according to Litta, two other daughters: Maria, who in 1483 married Giosué de Baenst, and Isabella, who in 1505 married Wulstaert van Lichtervelde.

6. Scholars have pondered whether the will's designation "sinte Franciscus in potrature" could conform to the iconography of the saint's stigmata. A more complex issue, however, is the problem of the *volets*. Henri Hymans ("Un tableau retrouvé de Jean van Eyck," *Bulletin des Commissions Royales d'Art et d'Archéologie*, vol. 22 [1883], pp. 108–16) pointed out discrepancies in the date of Marguerite van der Bank's death, variously reported as 1474 or 1462. See also Sterling, 1976, p. 56.

7. See Hymans, 1883, p. 114.

8. Ibid.

9. Friedländer, 1967, pp. 62–63; Aru and de Geradon, 1952, p. 9, speak of *un ancient religieux* and not of an *ex-religieuse*.

10. Massimo D'Azeglio was assisted by Luigi Gandolfi, who became director from 1866 to 1869. See P. Astrua, *Giovanni Vico e le collezioni torinesi di stampe e di libri figurati* (Turin, 1982–83).

11. Hymans, 1883, p. 116. The central *Annunciation* panel of the Rogier van der Weyden triptych, now dismantled, is in the Louvre and the wings are in the Galleria Sabauda, Turin (cat. nos. 189 and 190); see Martin Davies, *Rogier van der Weyden* (Milan, n.d.), pp. 227–28; and Riccardo Passoni, "Opere fiamminghe a Chieri," in *Arte del Quattrocento a Chieri*, ed. Michela di Macco and Giovanni Romano (Turin, 1988), pp. 67–97. See also the study of the old Flemish culture in the Piedmont area by P. Dardanello, "Il trittico fiammingo già a Villanova Mondovì," in *Ricerche sulla pittura del quattrocento in Piemonte, Strumenti per la didattica e la ricerca n. 3* (Turin, 1985), pp. 37–42.

12. According to A. Manno, *Il patriziato italiano, regione subalpina* (Florence, 1906), p. 8, one branch of the Adornos were lords of Castelletto d'Orba, which passed in 1617 to the Pallavicino-Adorno family; another branch, the principal one, ruled Silvano d'Orba, which passed to the Botta-Adorno family in 1613.

13. I believe that the date of "18th century," as reported by Hymans (1883, p. 115) in connection with the property of the ex-nun, is a typographical error; all the other texts agree on a timeframe of the nineteenth century. On the dispersal of ecclesiastical property in Alessandria in the nineteenth century, see Carlenrica Spantigati and G. Ieni, eds., *Pio V e Santa Croce di Bosco: Aspetti di una committenza papale* (Alessandria, 1985); and Spantigati and Giovanni Romano, eds., *Il Museo e la Pinacoteca di Alessandria* (Alessandria, 1986).

14. "Giornale Storico di Casale dall'anno 1785 al 1810 scritto dal casalese canonico G. de Conti," with a preface and notes by G. Giorcelli, in *Rivista di storia arte e archeologia per la provincia di Alessandria*, 1900, file 39, pp. 71–140. See the State Archives of Alessandria, Notarial Archive of Monferrato, bundle 4005, "Processi verbali di visita e descrizione dello Stato dei Conventi e Monasteri soppressi dell'anno undecimo della Repubblica Francese [1802]."

15. A detailed description of Casale prior to the suppression is provided by the *Ritratto della città di Casale scritto dal casalese canonico Giuseppe de Conti nell'anno 1794*, ed. G. Serraferro (Casale Monferrato, 1966).

16. Aru and de Geradon, 1952, p. 9.

17. See note 10; M. di Macco, in *Guida breve al patrimonio artistico delle provincie piemontesi* (Turin, 1979), pp. 75–92, esp. pp. 86–91.

18. Soprintendenza per i Beni Artistici e Storici di Torino, Vico file, L. inf. I/25.

19. I allude to the publication of the brother of Massimo, director of the Galleria from its inception in 1832 to 1854, Roberto D'Azeglio, *Notizie estetiche e biografiche sopra alcune precipue opere oltremontane del Museo Torinese* (Florence, 1962). See Spantigati, 1982; and Carlenrica Spantigati, "Vecchie e nuove precisazioni sulla quadreria del principe Eugenio di Savoia," in *Conoscere la Galleria Sabauda: Documenti sulla storia delle sue collezioni* (Turin, 1982), pp. 17–51.

20. *Guida ed indicazione sommaria dei quadri e dei capi d'arte della R. Pinacoteca di Torino*, rev. and ed., with an introduction by Francesco Gamba (Turin, 1883). Certainly Hymans, as he himself stated, was in direct contact with Gamba, but no correspondence between the two are retained in the Vico papers for the years 1882–83.

21. For a summary of the 1982 restoration, see "History of Modern Restorations" in this text.

22. See Sterling, 1976. Silvana Pettenati and A. Quazza have written on the history of the manuscript now in Turin and on the non-Eyckian miniatures, in E. Castelnuovo and Giovanni Romano, eds., *Giacomo Jacquerio e il gotico internazionale* (Turin, 1979), pp. 207–9; Pettenati, "L'emulazione verso i musei americani: gli acquisti dalle collezioni Gualino e Trivulzio, il Tesoro di Desana" in *Il Tesoro della Città*, ed. Silvana Pettenati and Giorgio Romano (Turin, 1996), pp. 187–203, esp. pp. 192–94; Anne Hagopian van Buren, James H. Marrow, and Silvana Pettenati, *Heures de Turin-Milan: Inv. No. 47, Museo Civico d'Arte Antica, Torino* (Lucerne, 1996). See also "The Philadelphia-Turin Paintings and the Turin-Milan Hours" by Maurits Smeyers in this volume.

23. Sterling, 1976, pp. 14–15.

24. Ibid., p. 56. This particular technique for protecting and decorating the back is also present on other Eyckian paintings, including the *Annunciation* panels of the Thyssen-Bornemisza Collection, Lugano.

25. The examination was completed in November 1985. The results of this examination have, of course, been made known by J.R.J. van Asperen de Boer, whom I thank along with Marigene Butler for our very useful exchange of ideas.

26. The restoration done by E. Patrito in the 1950s also examined the inscription, as documented by the photographic record of the operation. The mysterious inscription had been executed by the artist in the final stages of the painting and therefore could not be seen either with X-radiographs or with reflectographic examination. Gian Luigi Nicola tried—using a relief-pad procedure that he perfected—to gauge possible differences in the thickness of the paint surface in order to reconstruct the flow of strokes of the letters, but the scraped condition made this impossible.

27. See Aru and de Geradon, 1952, pp. 7, 9, with bibliography. The information usually supplied should be reversed: Saint Francis wears the traditional brown cowl, while it is Brother Leo who wears the gray robe.

28. Ibid.

29. Ibid., p. 11. See also J.R.J. van Asperen de Boer, "A Scientific Re-examination of the Ghent Altarpiece," *Oud Holland*, vol. 93, no. 3 (1979), p. 141 n. 4, pp. 204–5, 212.

30. In this connection the popularity enjoyed by the work in Spain is frequently cited, attested by, among other things, the early copy now in the Prado in Madrid (fig. 9). An Italian variation is documented by the drawings that G. B. Cavalcaselle derived in 1860 from a painting then in the church of San Francesco in Messina (destroyed by fire in 1884), which has been traditionally attributed to Salvo d'Antonio; see Paolini, 1980, p. 161.

31. Sterling, 1976, p. 29.

32. Ibid., p. 29, and fig. 37. However, for an opposing viewpoint, see "Geological Aspects of Jan van Eyck's 'Saint Francis Receiving the Stigmata'" by Kenneth Bé in this volume. Henri Hymans, "Le Saint François d'Assise de Jean van Eyck," *Gazette des Beaux-Arts*, 2nd period, vol. 37 (1888), pp. 78–83, identified the castle of Assisi in the view of the city in the background. In this connection, it should be remembered that in contemporary preaching and mod-

els of religious life, the theme of the stigmatization of Saint Francis was very closely associated with the Passion of Christ. Devotion to the Passion was encouraged in Europe with the construction of copies of sites in the Holy Land, the object of pilgrimages. The most famous was Sacro Monte of Varallo, which was the "new Jerusalem" of Father Bernardino Caimi (Guido Gentile, "Da Bernardino Caimi a Gaudenzio Ferrari: Immaginario e regia del Sacro Monte," *De Valle Sicida, Società Valsesiana di Cultura*, no. 1 [1996], pp. 207–87). In the 1430s construction of the Jeruzalemkapel, based on the Holy Sepulchre, was begun under the patronage of Pierre Adorno (J. Penninck, *De Jeruzalemkerk te Brugge* [Bruges, 1996]; A. Vandewalle, *Adornes en Jeruzalem: International levens in het 15de- en 16de-eeuwse Brugge*, September 9–23, 1983). Pierre had vowed to undertake a trip to Palestine, which his son Anselme accomplished in 1470.

33. Sterling, 1976, p. 29, stressed the ties existing at the time between the duke of Burgundy and the Franciscan order. Also Pierre Adorno could have been the patron; Anselme was too young at the time.

34. Especially Leonardo da Vinci, *Landscape*, 1473, pen and ink, Galleria degli Uffizi, Florence; see E. H. Gombrich, *The Heritage of Apelles: Studies in the Art of the Renaissance* (Ithaca, 1976), pp. 33–34, fig. 77.

35. Günter Panhans, "Florentiner Maler verarbeiten ein eyckisches Bild," *Wiener Jahrbuch für Kunstgeschichte*, vol. 27 (1974), pp. 188–98.

36. See Martin Davies, *National Gallery Catalogues: The Earlier Italian Schools*, 2nd ed. (London, 1961), pp. 97–98.

37. The "Italian" popularity of Van Eyck is amply attested by the early *De Viris Illustribus*, written in 1456 by Bartolomaeus Facius, secretary to Alfonso of Naples (see Michael Baxandall, "Bartholomaeus Facius on Painting: A Fifteenth-Century Manuscript of the *De Viris Illustribus*," *Journal of the Warburg and Courtauld Institutes*, vol. 27 [1964], pp. 102–3).

As far as Florence is concerned, the admiration expressed by Vasari is well known (Giorgio Vasari, *Le vite*, eds. P. Della Pergola, Luigi Grassi, and Giovanni Previtali [Novara, 1967], vol. 1, pp. 131–32, "Del dipingere ad olio . . . ," vol. 2, pp. 438–40, "Vita di Antonello da Messina," vol. 2, pp. 461–65, "Di diversi artefici fiamminghi"). For examples of Florentine imitations of Van Eyck, see Annarosa Garzelli, "Sulla fortuna del Gerolamo mediceo del Van Eyck nell'arte fiorentina del Quattrocento," in *Scritti in Storia dell'Arte in onore di Roberto Salvini* (Florence, 1984), pp. 347–53.

38. Heers and de Groer, 1978.

39. Sterling, 1976, p. 101.

40. The question is considered by August L. Mayer, "A Jan van Eyck Problem," *The Burlington Magazine*, vol. 48 (1926), p. 200. See also Friedländer, 1967, p. 63; and Aru and de Geradon, 1952, p. 7.

41. The drawing is certainly from late 1431 (see Faggin, 1968, no. 11), and the painting was therefore executed later.

42. This restoration was executed at an unspecified date, but believed to be shortly after the publication of Carlo Aru's study in 1952 (Aru and de Geradon, 1952).

Fig. 32. The John G.
Johnson Collection,
Philadelphia Museum of
Art *Saint Francis Receiving
the Stigmata* after 1989
treatment. Reproduced
actual size.

Marigene H. Butler

An Investigation of the Philadelphia "Saint Francis Receiving the Stigmata"

The technical investigation of the Philadelphia Museum of Art's *Saint Francis Receiving the Stigmata* in the John G. Johnson Collection (pl. I, fig. 32) began in 1983 in response to the College Art Association's session devoted to the picture and continued through its treatment, which was completed in 1989. The goals of the research were to learn as much as possible about its materials and technique as well as to pursue its relationship to the painting of the same subject—but approximately four times larger—in the collection of the Galleria Sabauda in Turin (pl. II).

Conservators, scientists, and art historians from the United States and Europe have collaborated on this project in an unusually productive manner, which will be illuminated by this publication. Investigative techniques have ranged from the use of low-powered stereomicroscopy and polarized-light microscopy to infrared reflectography, dendrochronology, and X-ray fluorescence. In addition, paintings by Jan van Eyck have been examined by the author with a stereomicroscope and infrared reflectography in London, Berlin, and Washington, D.C., along with related works in New York and Cleveland.[1]

During the course of the cleaning, many scholars studied the Johnson Collection picture in the laboratory, and their thoughtful comments contributed greatly to the investigation and treatment.[2] While the treatment of the picture in Philadelphia was in progress, it was particularly helpful to study the Turin painting several times in situ with the cooperation of the director of the Galleria Sabauda.[3]

The Materials of the Johnson Collection Painting
The painting's dimensions are as follows:

Design (not including border):
h. 4⅞" (12.4 cm)
w. 5¾" (14.6 cm)

Parchment (support for design and border):
h. 5¹⁄₁₆" (12.9 cm)
w. 6" (15.2 cm)

Panel:
left	h. 6¹⁄₁₆"	(15.4 cm)
right	h. 6"	(15.2 cm)
top	w. 6⁹⁄₁₆"	(16.7 cm)
bottom	w. 6⅝"	(16.85 cm)

The paint has been applied to a piece of parchment that has been glued to a wooden panel. The panel consists of five members; its conformation

can be studied most readily in the X-radiograph
(fig. 33). The central panel, approximately the
same size as the parchment, is oak, with the grain
running horizontally. Of radial cut, this panel
appears to have been carefully selected to mini-
mize warping. A top addition of oak with the
grain running vertically appears to be of an age
similar to the central member. A bottom addition
of oak with the grain running horizontally
appears to be newer. It is suspected that both the
top and bottom additions have been glued on
with an overlap of bevels on each member. This
cannot be determined for certain, but the overlap
of the top member's edge is suggested in the X-
radiographs, where one can see an overlap of
grains running perpendicular to one another.
The side additions are of beech and appear to be
more recent than the top and bottom additions.
They are butt-joined to the central panels and
have been nailed, and possibly glued, onto them.
The X-radiograph shows several types of nails.
The top left and right nails appear to have the
characteristics of machine-made wire nails and to
be more modern. The remaining nails show varying characteristics of both cut and wrought nails
and may date to the period when the technology
for machine-made nails was being developed,
about 1800.[4] In the X-radiograph, corrosion is
visible at the tips of the bottom-most nails on the
right and left sides, appearing as a blur at the tip
of each nail. All the nails are headless.

Fig. 33. X-radiograph of the Philadelphia *Saint Francis*.

All the additions have glue residues visible
on the reverse, with an imprint of fabric weave,
which may have resulted from ironing during
the gluing process. A filling material has been
casually applied on the reverse to level the joins
of the top and bottom members. A brown paint
of calcium carbonate, colored with brown and
red iron oxide pigments, applied to the reverse,
has been partially scraped off, especially over the
bottom addition, where it covers an earlier red,
vermilion-containing paint (fig. 34). A curving
crack or scratch runs horizontally across the
central panel and is visible in the X-radiograph,
probably as a result of having been filled with
paint, making it appear more dense.

Dendrochronological dating of the central
panel has been carried out by Peter Klein. His
examination, reported by him in full in this publication, indicates that the growth rings of the
tree from which it was cut can be dated between
1225 and 1307 in comparison with the master
chart of the Baltic/Polish region. He describes

Fig. 34. Reverse of the Philadelphia *Saint Francis*.

Fig. 35. Parchment visible beneath the red border, left vertical edge of the Philadelphia *Saint Francis*.

Fig. 36. Cross-section sample (h. 8.4 cm, w. 1.8 cm), magnified 136x, from the gray rocks at the left edge of the Philadelphia *Saint Francis*. The section shows the priming below two layers of paint.

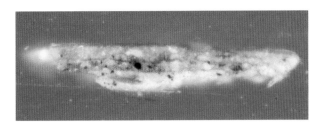

the growth ring curve of the Johnson Collection picture's central panel as identically matching the last part of the growth ring curve—and therefore from the same tree—as the panels of the portraits of Giovanni Arnolfini and Baudouin de Lannoy by Jan van Eyck, now in the Gemäldegalerie in Berlin (figs. 59, 60).[5]

Parchment serves as the primary support upon which a priming and the paint have been applied. One can follow the edge of the parchment via cracks along the vertical sides and across the upper edge of the top border. Excavation through layers of later paint revealed the bottom edge of the parchment beneath the red border (fig. 35). The parchment is estimated to be about 1 millimeter in thickness. This estimate is based upon a rough measurement of a small section of the parchment's edge, which is visible at the top right corner of the red border. The measurement of 1 millimeter is considerably thicker than the 0.1 to 0.2 millimeter thickness of pages of manuscripts contemporary with Van Eyck. However, the thicker parchment of the *Saint Francis* might well have been considered to be a more appropriate support for an oil painting.

Fibers were teased out from the exposed edge of the parchment along the left vertical crack, mounted, and viewed using a polarized-light microscope. The fibers compared positively with a mounted reference sample of parchment viewed under similar conditions with the microscope.[6] The parchment support is brownish gray in color. Its tightly intermeshed fibers suggest that the paint may have been applied to the "grain" or hair side of the parchment, which would have a lower grease content.[7] The preparation of parchment normally included a smoothing process, sometimes accomplished by rubbing with glass-containing bread;[8] this may account for the minute, glasslike particles that appear in the priming layer and in some of the paint mixtures (see Appendix 1). When dilute hydrochloric acid is added to the sampled fibers (as viewed through the low-powered stereomicroscope), bubbles form, suggesting the presence of calcium car-

bonate particles, which may have been used to de-grease or whiten the parchment, or influence its drying time during preparation.

A single layer of pinkish tan priming has been thinly applied to the surface of the parchment. It lies under both the image and fragments of a border that encircles the image area. The priming layer measures 8 to 16 μm (1 micrometer = approx. 1/25,000 inch) in thickness and is so thin that it is visible only in highly magnified cross sections (fig. 36). The thinness of the priming layer suggests that it may have been applied simply to fill the interstices of the parchment and to provide a smooth surface suitable to receive minute brush strokes of paint, yet thin enough not to crack as the parchment expanded and contracted in response to changes in the relative humidity of its environment. The priming contains:

20% calcium carbonate
40% lead white
10% iron oxide yellow
10% charcoal black
20% glasslike particles

The medium of the priming is insoluble in water and dissolves slowly in dilute sodium hydroxide, suggesting that it is oil.[9]

The priming appears to have adhered well to the parchment. However, where there are flake losses of paint, the priming is generally also missing, for example, on Saint Francis's temple.

In contrast to the priming on the parchment, a quite different material has been used for the ground that covers the added pieces of wood on all four sides of the central panel. A single thick, white layer, consisting of 100% calcium carbonate (chalk), has been applied as a ground. This material is readily dissolved by water, suggesting a glue medium. It has been applied in a thick layer that carries over the edge of the parchment in some places, resulting in a different plane from that on which the original design is painted.

The paint is soluble in dilute sodium hydroxide solution but not in water, strongly suggesting that it is oleaginous. The paint has been thinly applied in paste vehicular mixtures in layers ranging from 6 to 15 μm in thickness, insofar as measurements were possible, given the very few cross sections taken due to the small size of the painting. The pigments, as identified by polarized-light microscopy (see

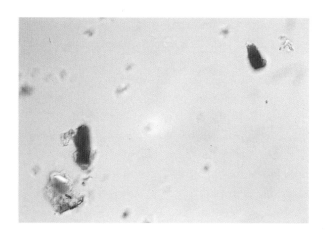

Appendix 1),[10] and confirmed by X-ray fluorescence (see Appendix 2)[11] include:

chalk (calcium carbonate), $CaCO_3$
lead white (basic lead carbonate), $2PbCO_3 \cdot Pb(OH)_2$
vermilion (mercuric sulfide), HgS
iron oxide red (ferric oxide), Fe_2O_3
red lake, unidentified organic dye
iron oxide yellow (hydrated ferric oxide), $Fe_2O_3 \cdot H_2O$
lead tin yellow (lead tin oxide), Pb_2SnO_4
copper-resinate green (copper salts of resin acids), $C_{19}H_{29}COOH$
natural ultramarine (lapis lazuli), $3Na_2O \cdot 3Al_2O_3 \cdot 6SiO_2 \cdot 2Na_3S$
charcoal black, (C)

In addition to the above pigments, as noted earlier, about 20% of the priming sample consists of silica or glasslike particles, which may result from the preparation of the parchment support. Small quantities of these particles are present in the samples taken from the flesh tone, yellow flower, blue wing, and gray rock. In the minute quantity of blue sampled from the seraph's wing, mounted in Aroclor® medium with a refractive index of 1.66, the particles of ultramarine (refractive index 1.51) bore the characteristics of natural ultramarine, that is, medium to deep blue color in 3 to 18 μm particles, tabular in shape with smooth surfaces and jagged, glasslike fracture and cleavage along the edges (fig. 37). Particles of calcium carbonate were associated with the nearly pure ultramarine content of the sample.

Technique of the Johnson Collection Painting
Underdrawing is not generally visible with infrared reflectography in this painting, although, with solvent and magnification, a few strokes appear to be visible on Saint Francis's robe, just below the right sleeve. Most of the drawing that models the form has been applied with fine brush strokes of paint upon the surface of the base layer of paint, for example, to indicate the folds in Saint Francis's robe (fig. 38).

Generally, a single layer of paint has been applied in a given design area and an additional layer has then been used to indicate highlights, shadows, and details. For example, the flesh tones have been painted with a base layer of vermilion in lead white. The proportion of vermilion increases in Saint Francis's rosy cheek. Upon this base layer, strokes of white and light pink indicate highlights, while strokes of pure vermilion indicate wrinkles on the hands and are used in hatch lines to indicate shadows on the side of the proper right foot. A dark brown paint mixture has been applied with very fine parallel strokes to model the eyes and ear and to outline the perimeters of hands and feet. The stigmata have been applied in a red organic lake. On the face a stubble of beard is indicated with a stippling of blue and brown hues. A similar dotting can be

Fig. 39. Detail of the Philadelphia *Saint Francis*.

distinguishable only with magnification, have been applied parallel to one another to construct thicker lines. Brother Leo's gray robe has been painted in much the same way, with the form modeled in delicate dark gray strokes laid upon a medium gray base tone.

The rocks are painted in similar fashion. At the left, a base tone of light gray to brown to dark gray has been laid on first. Upon this, a few rust-colored accent strokes have been applied and the complex forms of the rocks modeled with dark gray and black strokes (fig. 40). At the right side, the base rock tone varies from warm yellow-tan to shrimp-tan hues. Over this, forms are modeled with a few pinkish orange and white highlight tones, brown-black lines and dark gray washes. White and pink paint mixtures are used on the surface to indicate the presence of fossils in the rocks.

The greenery includes foreground grasses and flowers, midground shrubbery, and distant trees. All make use of what is apparently a copper-resinate green that has turned brown, judging from the appearance of samples in polarized light (fig. 41) and the copper present in X-ray fluorescence analyses of the green and brown foliage areas (see Appendix 2). In the foreground, an opaque base layer of green contains lead tin yellow and flakes of copper-resinate green in lead white. This has been used to depict grasses and small plants of various types. A copper-resinate glaze applied over the base green has discolored to a semitransparent brown. In the middle distance, trees are painted with black trunks, opaque green-dotted highlights, and resinous dark brown shadow areas. The distant trees and shrubs are painted solely with a copper-containing, semitransparent resinous material, now turned brown (fig. 42).

In the cityscape, blue shadows and black windows have been applied over the base white of the buildings. Beyond the city, the distant mountains have been painted with varying amounts of natural ultramarine in lead white. The sky has been painted with pure lead white at the horizon and also in the clouds, which are textured with brush marking. Small amounts of ultramarine blue in lead white comprise the blue sky tint.

The pigment mixtures used for painting different tones are listed on the attached pigment tables (Appendix 1).

The simple application of paint, using one

Fig. 40. Detail of the rocks at the left side of the Philadelphia *Saint Francis*, showing painting technique.

seen in shadow areas around the proper right eye of Saint Francis. The white of the eye is painted with a few particles of ultramarine in lead white (fig. 39).

Saint Francis's robe has been laid in with a base layer, modulated from tan gray in highlight areas through medium gray to brown paint in shadow areas. Over this base tone a dark brown-black paint has been used to model form. In the process of modeling, many very fine strokes,

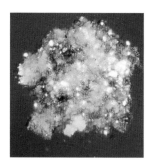

Fig. 41. Pigment sample (h. 8.9 cm, w. 4.8 cm) with copper-resinate green and lead tin yellow, magnified 312x, from the greenery of the Philadelphia *Saint Francis*.

Fig. 42. Detail of the trees and shrubs painted with copper-containing resinous material in the Philadelphia *Saint Francis*.

Fig. 43. Detail of the cityscape in the Philadelphia *Saint Francis*.

or two layers, is appropriate to the small size of this painting and differs from the multiple layers found in larger, more complex Eyckian paintings, such as the Ghent altarpiece, where the large scale permits a more complicated modeling of form.[12]

When studying the Johnson Collection painting, the use of magnification enhances appreciation of the incredible detail and the similarity of its brushwork to that seen more readily in the larger Turin painting. With magnification, one can see the tiny figures of animals, or people making their way along paths on the distant hillside or engaged in commercial activity along the city wall at center (fig. 43). The vigorous brush strokes used to paint the clouds and the white peaks of the mountains have created a lively texture in the white paint in those areas in the small painting (fig. 44). Wildflowers, which are easy to distinguish in the Turin painting can, with magnification, be seen to have been depicted in complete, although minute detail in the Johnson painting, using exactly the same language of brush strokes as in the larger painting (fig. 45). What appears to the naked eye in the Johnson painting to be a single, delicate brown line defining form in Saint Francis's fingers or in the folds of his robe, can, with magnification, be seen to consist of a succession of extremely delicate strokes, similar to the hatching of the Eyckian underdrawing in the Turin picture (fig. 46) and in other paintings by Jan van Eyck. One concludes that some form of magnification must have been used by the painter who created the Johnson painting.

Border of the Johnson Collection Painting
A casually applied red border surrounds the image on all four edges. Cross sections indicate that the stratigraphy of the border differs from one edge to another. Across the bottom edge and along both sides, a layer of gold leaf lies on a pale cream-yellow preparation over the tan priming. The gold border extends from the outer edge of the parchment into the edge of the design area (about .3 cm). At the inner edge

Fig. 44. Detail of the clouds and mountain peaks of the Philadelphia *Saint Francis*, showing vigorous brushwork in the white pigment.

Fig. 45. Comparative detail of the distant landscape on the left of the Turin *Saint Francis*.

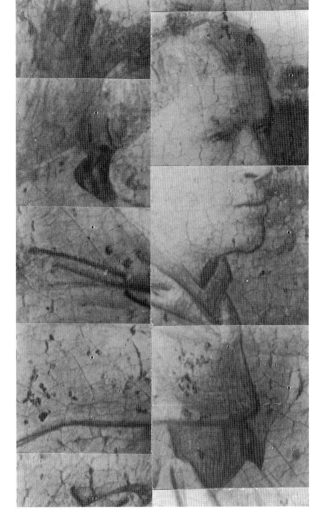

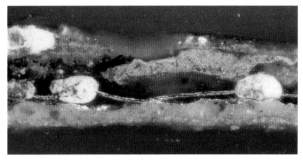

Fig. 48. Cross section (h. 12.1 cm, w. 1.4 cm) from the left
vertical border, magnified 136x, of the Philadelphia *Saint
Francis*, showing gold over a preparation layer covered by
opaque orange red and red lake layers.

of the left border, the gold is covered with a
dark red-brown resinous or lake layer (fig. 47).
Cross sections from the outer edge of the left
side, and similarly on the bottom edge and right
side, indicate a separation of layers above the
gold followed by an opaque orange-red layer
and then a red lake layer, possibly part of a later
marbleizing scheme (fig. 48). Another separation between layers follows on the side and bottom edges and then a succession of white and
gray layers, culminating in the presently visible
orange red. It is possible that each of the separa-
tions between layers in the cross sections corre-
lates with a time lapse between border schemes,
the succession of which follows:

1. Gold leaf, with dark red inner edge only on
   the left border.
2. Marbleized orange red and red lake.
3. The present orange red.

The top border's stratigraphy is different. After
cleaning, traces of an original gold border over
a cream-colored preparation could be seen
using a low-powered stereomicroscope at five

points across the top edge, laid over original
blue sky paint. The gold was glazed with dark
red lake, similar to the system found in the left
border. The original border system thus
appears to have copied the shadow effect of the
top and left borders often used in manuscript
illuminations. Outside the traces of the original
border, a greenish blue pigment, containing
Prussian blue, which came into use only after
1750,[13] lies over a translucent tan ground. In
places, above the blue, are several layers of the
orange red that is found as the top layer on the
other three sides, indicating a more modern
application of paint.

*State of Preservation of the
Johnson Collection Painting*

In general, the paint is in good condition. An
irregular net, mechanical age fracture crackle
has formed in the paint. Crackle lines vary in
size, with larger lines outlining the irregular net
pattern and many smaller lines lying within the
larger pattern. The entire crackle system is
appropriate to a paint film responding to the
expansion and contraction of a parchment support and does not have the rectilinear conformation of a paint film responding to a wooden support. This suggests that the crackle formed
before the parchment was mounted on the
wooden panel, but might simply indicate that
the forces for expansion and contraction within
the parchment were stronger than those in the
panel.[14] In contrast, the more recent discolored
natural resin varnish, recently removed, had a
rectilinear crackle pattern, suggesting that it had
formed when the painting was subject to expansion and contraction forces of the wooden
panel. The gray robe has a minute traction or
drying crackle overall, which may have caused

Fig. 49. The Philadelphia *Saint Francis* before cleaning (December 15, 1982).

the uneven surface and seemingly poorer condition of the paint in this area.

The History of Treatment of the Johnson Collection Painting

In 1906, after the painting was acquired by John G. Johnson, Roger Fry carried out what was evidently an extensive restoration treatment. This is documented briefly in a note that appeared in *The Burlington Magazine* in May 1926, where Fry described the removal of extensive overpaints, which revealed that an "extra piece had been added on" to the top and that "a brilliant scarlet margin" surrounded the original panel. "When it came to me, the panel was considerably larger at the top, and a dull, opaque sky concealed the join where the extra piece had been added on to satisfy some owner who did not appreciate the compressed composition of the original. The sky had been enlivened, if I remember right, with a crowd of small white, cloud-like forms suggesting the presence of a cohort of angels. These all came away with the sky and then, to my surprise, I found that the original panel appeared surrounded by a brilliant scarlet margin, painted on the panel, just as might have been seen on the border of a manuscript illumination."[15]

The wording of Fry's note suggests that he may have been responsible for reducing the added top portion of the panel in size.

The only other recorded treatment of this painting is the one completed by the author in 1989, which had been ongoing for several years during the course of the research project. Following a thorough technical investigation, the painting was cleaned (fig. 49). A natural resin varnish, which had turned dark brown, was removed first, using tiny, toothpick-sized swabs with acetone and working under the stereomicroscope. The slow solubility of the varnish film suggested that it had some oil content. This was followed by mechanical removal of old filling and retouching materials from around the inner edge of the border. These materials were easily identifiable by their large agglomerates of lead white and larger particle sizes than the original paint. These mixtures also contained viridian, a pigment not readily available until after 1859.[16]

Fig. 50. The Philadelphia *Saint Francis* after cleaning, before inpainting (January 4, 1989).

Next, an oil film that had discolored to a dark yellow was reduced or removed, greatly enhancing the sense of distance in the composition. Beneath the oil film lay old tannish gray fillings, evidently applied to level out a drying crackle that had formed in Brother Leo's gray robe. The overpaints covering these fills were removed, and the fillings reduced so that they no longer covered original paint. The modeling of the gray robe was revealed to be quite intact, so that the three-dimensional form of the figure could be appreciated once more. Finally, old yellowed overpaints were removed from the distant white-capped mountain peaks. These may have been applied at some time in the past to cover discolored varnish residues that had collected in depressions in the very lively brushwork of the original paint, which lay intact below. Overpaints on Saint Francis's head were also removed, revealing a tonsure at the very back of the head. Overpaints were also removed from the rocks at the upper right, revealing an X scratched irregularly into the surface of the original paint. This damage can be seen in the after-cleaning-before-inpainting photograph (fig. 50).

When the cleaning had been completed, the painting received a series of isolating varnish coatings consisting of a synthetic polycyclohexanone resin with 1% microcrystalline wax to achieve a saturation of the paint surface. The very small amount of inpainting required was carried out using dry pigments ground in a polyvinyl acetate resin, followed by a final protective layer of the same varnish that was used in the isolating layer.

Removal of all of the later additions revealed the original paint to be in amazingly good condition. There are losses on Saint Francis's forehead and temple, minute losses in Brother Leo's gray robe, and losses in the sky along the top edge where the edge of the parchment support is somewhat jagged and uneven. Otherwise, the original paint is intact and one can once again appreciate the quality of the brushwork and the precision of rendering of detail, for example, the naturalistic depiction of rocks, plants, and water in the stream (fig. 51). Removal of the veils of discolored, later films has enabled the recession of planes in space to once again become visible as the viewer's eye is led down from the mountaintop, across the valley, to the distant snow-capped mountains.

Comparison of the Johnson Collection Painting with the Turin Painting

Although the design and subject matter of both paintings are nearly identical, differences between the two have been observed, not only in scale, but also in materials, technique, and color. Oil paint applied to a parchment support in the Johnson picture contrasts with the application of oil paint applied directly to a primed panel in the Turin picture. Although rare, other examples of oil on parchment have survived, such as the Petrus Christus *Head of Christ* in the collection of the Metropolitan Museum of Art, New York.[17]

J.R.J. van Asperen de Boer describes elsewhere in this publication the extensive Eyckian underdrawing in the Turin painting, which has been revealed by infrared reflectography, as compared with only a few possible strokes seen in the Philadelphia painting.

Review at the Institut Royal du Patrimoine Artistique in Brussels in 1988 of several surviving pigment samples taken from the Turin painting in 1949 by Paul Coremans indicated a simple paint structure with a chalk/glue ground and one or two paint layers, unlike the more complex structures found in other paintings by Jan van Eyck sampled by that laboratory.[18] An incomplete list of pigments includes lead white, red earth, ultramarine, and black. The Turin chalk/glue ground differs from the toned lead white priming found in the Johnson picture. The paint mixtures in the Turin painting appear to have been applied in thicker layers with rougher surfaces and larger pigment particle sizes than those found in the Johnson painting.

The tonalities of parts of the Turin painting are, in general, lighter and paler than those of the Johnson painting. For example, in the Turin painting, the rocks in the right background are light gray with a few rust-colored strokes, whereas in the Johnson painting the same rocks are more orange tan. Similarly, the copper-resinate greens in the foreground of the Turin painting are paler and cooler than in the Johnson painting, where they are a darker, brownish green, probably resulting from discoloration of

the copper-resinate green there. It has been speculated that the very thin layers of paint of the smaller painting, applied over parchment, may have permitted more penetration of light through the resinous greens, resulting in more severe discoloration of the copper-resinate greens to their present brownish tone.[19] Because the paint layers in the Johnson picture are so thin, care might have been taken to avoid use of a black underdrawing material, which would have been difficult to hide under thin, semi-transparent layers of paint such as would have been used in working in the small scale of the Johnson painting.

Volumes in the Turin painting are modeled up in paint from the underdrawing, while in the Philadelphia painting volumes are often defined through the use of discrete lines on the surface of the base paint layer, or in a series of fine par-

Fig. 51. Detail of the rocks, plants, and stream in the Philadelphia *Saint Francis*.

Fig. 52. Detail of the rocks in the right background of the Philadelphia *Saint Francis*, showing dark lines defining the rocks.

Fig. 53. Detail of the hands of Saint Francis in the Philadelphia *Saint Francis*, with minute hatching lines modeling the fingers.

allel hatching lines on the surface. Examples can be seen in the dark lines that define the rocks at the right background (fig. 52) or, as mentioned earlier, in the minute, parallel hatching lines that model the fingers of Saint Francis's hands in the smaller painting (fig. 53). With magnification, these hatching strokes on the surface of the paint can be seen to be similar in conformation to the delicate hatching strokes seen in the underdrawing on reflectograms of the Turin painting, or in the underdrawing of the Ghent altarpiece.[20]

Much of the difference in technique may result from the Johnson painting's very much smaller size, only one quarter the area of the Turin painting, so that various aspects of form are necessarily abbreviated in the smaller painting. As a result of the differences in technique because of the differences in scale, the Turin painting appears to be more naturalistic in some of its detail than the Johnson painting, for example, in the modeling of the rocks in the background.

The two pictures' identical designs and subject matter and nearly identical proportions can be confirmed by projecting an image of one painting onto an image of the other. When this is done, the proportions of individual parts of the composition match quite precisely but cannot all be aligned simultaneously. If the figures are lined up, the rocks are slightly out of register. Alternatively, if the landscape elements are lined up, the figures are slightly out of register. This may be the result of the design's having been transferred by means of patterns or some other technique from the painting in Turin to the parchment upon which the Johnson picture has been painted.

In the Turin painting, the figures appear to have more volume and to be more completely integrated into the spatial organization as planes recede into space. In contrast, in the Johnson painting, the figures of Saint Francis and Brother Leo appear slightly flattened and as if positioned on the foreground plane, somewhat separated from the planes of the landscape that recede behind them.

The most notable similarity between the two paintings can be seen in the brushwork and the manner in which paint is laid upon the surface of the supports. In both paintings, a semi-transparent veil of white paint is used in areas of highlight to model form, for example, in the flesh tones and on the surface of the rocks. Using magnification, one can see that flowers and blades of grass in the foreground are painted using the identical language of brush strokes in both paintings. Similarly, the clouds and the snow-covered mountain peaks in both paintings are painted with the same lively brush strokes that have left a textured surface in the paint film. Although the faces of the two Saint Francis figures depict two different individuals, the brushwork used on both is identical, whether to model the eye sockets or to depict wrinkles on the brow or stubble on the chin. The viewer can only conclude that either the same hand applied the paint in both paintings or that two artists, working in such close collaboration that they used the same language of strokes, created the two paintings. Thus, if both paintings came from the same workshop, the only difference may lie in how much of each the master painted and how much an assistant might have painted. Recent research illuminates the close working relationships within a master's workshop and the extent to which assistants were expected to use brushwork and handle paint in a manner identical to that of their master's.[21]

It is possible that the Johnson Collection picture was commissioned in its small, light form by the owner of the larger picture to carry for personal worship while traveling, for example, on a pilgrimage to Jerusalem.

Comparison of Technique with
Other Paintings by Jan van Eyck

In trying to better understand the origins of the Johnson Collection painting, it has been helpful to compare its technique, especially its brushwork, with paintings that are firmly attributed to Jan van Eyck. As part of this effort, the *Portrait of a Young Man* (fig. 54) and *Man with a Turban* (fig. 55) in the National Gallery in London, and the *Portrait of Giovanni Arnolfini* (fig. 59) and the *Portrait of Baudouin de Lannoy* (fig. 60) in the Gemäldegalerie in Berlin were examined by the author with a low-powered stereomicroscope and infrared reflectography in the conservation laboratories of those institutions. Underdrawing was readily visible only in the *Portrait of Baudouin de Lannoy*, where the shadows on the sides of the face and neck are underdrawn with fine parallel strokes of typically Eyckian character (fig. 56). In the three other portraits, form tends to be modeled upon the surface of the base layer of paint, for example, in the *Portrait of a Young Man* and in the *Portrait of Baudouin de Lannoy* one can see that the fingers on the proper right hands are modeled with a succession of fine strokes applied to the surface of the base flesh tone layer of paint. In the *Man with a Turban*, fine, semitransparent strokes laid on the paint surface can be seen, with magnification, to define the form of the eyes, nose, and proper

left temple. This is similar to the technique used in the Johnson Collection *Saint Francis Receiving the Stigmata*, and described earlier, where the form of the robes and the rocks is modeled using very fine strokes of a shadow or highlight tone laid upon the surface of a base layer of paint. The use of this particular technique for modeling form may have been dictated by the small scale of both portraits and the Johnson painting, where more complicated layering of paint and working up of form becomes impossible due to lack of space. Only when one examines the Johnson painting using magnification can the individual, minute, delicate strokes of paint be distinguished and fully appreciated.

Jan van Eyck's painting *The Annunciation* (fig. 57), in the collection of the National Gallery of Art in Washington, D.C., is on a larger scale with a more complex system of layering of paint, yet its brushwork evidences similarities to the smaller paintings discussed above. Although this painting has extensive underdrawing,[22] minute brush strokes are used to further model form on the surface of the paint. Since the painting's recent cleaning, one can see, with a low-powered microscope, the extensive use of tiny, delicate strokes.[23] For example, a succession of fine brown strokes is used to model the roundness at the base of the Virgin's thumb, as well as her fingers. Her eye sockets are similarly

Fig. 54. Jan van Eyck, *Portrait of a Young Man*, panel, 13⅛ x 7½" (33.4 x 19 cm), National Gallery, London, no. 290.

Fig. 55. Jan van Eyck, *Man with a Turban*, panel, 10⅛ x 7½" (25.7 x 19 cm), National Gallery, London, no. 222.

Fig. 56. Infrared reflectogram assembly of the *Portrait of Baudouin de Lannoy*, Gemäldegalerie, Staatliche Museen zu Berlin Preussischer Kulturbesitz, Berlin (see fig. 60), showing fine parallel strokes of Eyckian character in the underdrawing.

cheeks, the tan of the shadows, and the cream of the mid-tone of highlights, with a white highlight applied last. The dark red lake of the angel's robe similarly consists of a succession of individual strokes applied with a very small brush.

In regard to the presence of underdrawing in portrait paintings by Jan van Eyck, J.R.J. van Asperen de Boer has observed that when Van Eyck painted without the sitter present, he did a careful portrait drawing from the sitter, which was then transferred in abbreviated fashion to the panel with hatching lines only to indicate the shadows.[24] In contrast, when he painted with the sitter present, he omitted the careful hatching lines from the panel. Such a practice may explain the limited amount of underdrawing in the three portraits discussed above. Similarly, in regard to the Saint Francis paintings, if Jan van Eyck were painting a second version of an earlier painting executed by himself, he might have found it unnecessary to create a detailed underdrawing for it.

Comparison with Eyckian Miniatures in the Turin-Milan Hours

It is interesting to compare the Johnson Collection painting with the illumination *Christ in the Garden of Gethsemane* from the Turin-Milan Hours in the Museo Civico d'Arte Antica in Turin (fig. 108). Of all of the Eyckian illuminations in the manuscript, this one is most like the Johnson Collection *Saint Francis* in the realism with which the figures are depicted in the landscape. The faces are those of individual human beings, not painted by convention; the robes are modeled with three-dimensional form and realistic folds, and the planes recede into the distant landscape. The trees in the background are depicted with detail similar to those in the *Saint Francis*.

When the miniatures from the manuscript were examined with infrared reflectography, *Christ in the Garden of Gethsemane* showed considerable underdrawing of Eyckian character, especially in the rocks and in portions of the robes of the apostles (fig. 58).[25] In addition to the underdrawing, some of the lines indicating form appear to have been applied upon the surface of the base layer of paint in the same manner as those of the Johnson Collection painting: for example, black lines on the surface of the blue paint help to define the form of the folds of the blue robe of the middle apostle. The miniature evidences the

modeled with a series of fine, light brown strokes, and the wrinkles under her chin are created by a succession of fine brownish pink strokes that combine into stronger lines. The flesh tones on the face appear to be comprised of a web of tiny strokes going in every direction, and the paint layer is built up in thin veils of different hues of paint brushed one into another, wet into wet, for example, the rose of the dryness of the water-based medium of an illumination rather than the richness of oil paint; however, the paint appears to have been applied with somewhat more complex brushwork and layering than is found in the typical miniature illumination.

Conclusion

As J.R.J. van Asperen de Boer notes elsewhere in this publication, the Turin painting clearly has underdrawing similar to the underdrawing observed in autograph paintings by Jan van Eyck, such as the Ghent altarpiece. It therefore may well be one of the two pictures of Saint Francis by the hand of Jan van Eyck mentioned in the will of Anselme Adornes in 1470.[26]

Despite the fact that it is painted on parchment, the Philadelphia painting appears not to have come from a manuscript. Its oil medium in both paint and priming as well as the lead-white composition of the priming differ from the water-soluble medium and calcium carbonate priming typically used in illuminations. In addition, the Philadelphia picture is painted not by the conventions of manuscript illumination, but like the Turin picture, with such careful observation and rendering of naturalistic detail that one can only speculate that Jan van Eyck must have traveled through the Alps and seen with his own eyes jagged mountain peaks, gray rocks streaked with orange, small streams flowing through the rocks, distant white-capped peaks, and diversity of wildflowers that are rendered so specifically in the Johnson and Turin paintings.

Because the quality of the application of paint in the Philadelphia painting is so high, and the brushwork so similar to that of the Turin painting, it is difficult to believe it could be a copy by any hand other than the one that created the Turin painting. Except for size, the primary difference in the two images is in the depiction of the features of Saint Francis. Each rendering appears to be the portrait of a real person, clearly focused inward on an especially moving spiritual experience—surely appropriate images to have been intended for use in personal devotion. The fact that the wood panel support comes from the same tree as two other panels produced in the Van Eyck workshop places the Philadelphia painting very close to Jan van Eyck in its creation, and if not by the hand of the master himself, then by one trained in his workshop who worked closely with him.

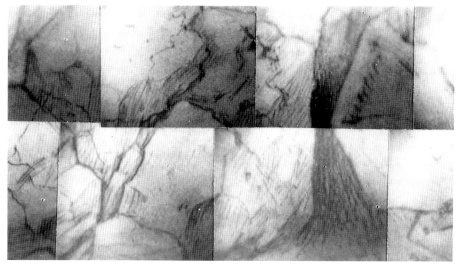

Fig. 58. Infrared reflectogram assembly from 1985 by J.R.J. van Asperen de Boer of *Christ in the Garden of Gethsemane*, illuminated page from the Turin-Milan Hours, Museo Civico d'Arte Antica, Turin (see fig. 108), showing underdrawing of Eyckian character in the boulders and in portions of the apostle's robes.

APPENDIX I

Dispersed pigment samples of the Philadelphia *Saint Francis* (John G. Johnson Collection, cat. 314)

Ground under gray rocks (h. 8.4 cm, w. 1.8 cm)
    parchment fibers
    20% calcium carbonate
    40% lead white
    10% iron oxide yellow
    10% charcoal black
    20% glasslike particles

Shrimp tone, rocks (h. 8.3 cm, w. 14.2 cm)
    10% calcium carbonate
    40% lead white
    30% vermilion
    10% iron oxide yellow
    5% natural ultramarine (grayed blue)
    5% charcoal black

Flesh tone, foot (h. 5.6 cm, w. 2.5 cm)
    85% lead white
    15% vermilion
    glasslike particles

Yellow, flower (h. 13.8 cm, w. 14.6 cm)
    5% calcium carbonate
    15% lead white
    80% lead tin yellow
    glasslike particles

Green, grass (h. 8.9 cm, w. 4.8 cm)
    10% lead white
    45% lead tin yellow
    45% copper-resinate green

Green, trees in midground (h. 11.0 cm, w. 4.5 cm)
    10% lead white
    30% lead tin yellow
    60% copper-resinate green

Green brown, tree in left background (h. 13.2 cm, w. 2.8 cm)
    25% lead tin yellow
    75% copper-resinate green

APPENDIX 2

Analysis report, January 12, 1987, of the National Gallery of Art, Washington, D.C., for the Philadelphia *Saint Francis* (John G. Johnson Collection, cat. 314). The painting was brought to the Science Department of the National Gallery of Art, on October 22, 1986, in order to study the elemental composition of pigmented areas. This information was requested to confirm microscopic examination and identification of pigments.

Energy dispersive X-ray fluorescence, a nondestructive technique, was used with the following conditions: Kevex 0750A, $BaCl_2$ secondary target, 50 kV and 1 mA; 6 mm source collimator and 2 mm detector collimator, 300 second live time, except for spectra I, J, and K, where a Mo secondary target, 40 kV and 1.5 mA was used.

The following list provides information on the elemental composition for the areas tested:

Location	*Elemental Composition*
Tree (A)	Pb, *Sn*, *Cu*, (Fe), *Ca*
Angel wing (B)	Pb, (Cu), (Ca), (Sn)
White beneath wing (C)	Pb, (Fe)
Trees (D)	Pb, Cu, (Fe), (Ca), *Sn*
Green above grass (E)	Pb, *Cu*, (Fe), *Ca*, *Sn*
Yellow flower (F)	Pb, *Cu*, *Ca*, (Fe), *Sn*
Red line on rock (G)	Pb, (Fe), (Ca), (Sn)
Red on cross (H)	Pb, (Cu), (Fe), (Ca), (Sn)
Viridian in sky (I)	Pb, *Fe*, (Cr), (Ca), (Hg)
Blue on added strip (J)	Pb, (Fe), *Ca*, (Hg)
Rock (K)	Pb, *Cu*, *Fe*, (Ca)

Note: Unannotated elemental symbol indicates a major peak in spectrum; *italic* denotes a minor peak in spectrum; (parentheses) denote a trace peak in spectrum.

Blue, sky (h. 13.6 cm, w. 1.2 cm)
    85% lead white
    15% natural ultramarine

Blue, wing (h. 12.9 cm, w. 11.3 cm)
    15% calcium carbonate
    70% natural ultramarine
    15% glasslike particles

Gray, rocks (h. 8.2 cm, w. 1.7 cm)
    30% calcium carbonate
    40% lead white
     5% iron oxide red
    10% iron oxide yellow
    15% charcoal black
        glasslike particles

1. Through the courtesy of Alistair Smith and Martin Wyld at the National Gallery, London, the Jan van Eyck paintings *Portrait of a Young Man* (fig. 54) and *Man with a Turban* (fig. 55) were examined in September 1987 by the author in the laboratory with a low-powered stereomicroscope and viewed with infrared reflectography with the assistance of David Bomford. Similarly, due to the kindness of Henning Bock and Rainald Grosshans, the *Portrait of Giovanni Arnolfini* and the *Portrait of Baudouin de Lannoy* (figs. 59, 60) in the Gemäldegalerie in Berlin were examined in September 1988 by the author with a low-powered stereomicroscope in the laboratory and examined with infrared reflectography with the assistance of Gerald Schultz. All four portraits have varying degrees of discolored varnishes and old retouchings, making it difficult to sort out all aspects of the designs, however, with a stereomicroscope some original brushwork could be identified and studied in each picture.

Through the kindness of David Bull, the author was able to examine *The Annunciation* by Jan van Eyck (fig. 57), on two occasions in the laboratory of the National Gallery of Art, Washington, D.C., with a stereomicroscope: on January 22, 1986, before the painting was cleaned, and on April 3, 1992, during the course of treatment.

On December 2, 1985, the author was able to participate in Maryan Ainsworth's and Katherine Crawford's infrared reflectography overall scanning of the Eyckian diptych panels *The Crucifixion* (fig. 21) and *The Last Judgment* (33.92b) at the Metropolitan Museum of Art, New York. Underdrawing in very small strokes was revealed overall on both panels, requiring positioning of the vidicon very close to the panel in order to distinguish the strokes. However, the drawing differed from one panel to the other. The underdrawing of *The Crucifixion* in delicate, parallel hatching strokes defines form and indicates a few changes in design. The expressions on the underdrawn faces are both individual and human. The underdrawing in the upper portions of the *Last Judgment* appears to be by a different hand however—rougher, more crude, and guided more by convention than by intellect—compared to *The Crucifixion*. The underdrawing also appears to be less sure, with many more changes than in the other panel. In the lower parts of the panel, the underdrawing is more typical, with fine lines; however, these strokes are more at random and less meticulous than in *The Crucifixion*. For example, the underdrawing lines create patches of shade but do not define form.

The painting *John the Baptist in a Landscape*, circle of Jan van Eyck (fig. 123), was examined at the Cleveland Museum of Art on October 23, 1985, by Joseph Rishel and the author through the kindness of Evan Turner and Bruce Miller. Seen through the low-powered stereomicroscope, the pigment mixtures are more particulate, with large dark particles, than those of the Johnson Collection *Saint Francis*, and the technique, more painterly with blending of tones (for example in the roofs) and a greater sequence of tones. The foreground grasses and flowers are similar to the *Saint Francis* but the face is more abbreviated, as are the buildings.

2. Scholars who have examined the Johnson Collection painting in the conservation laboratory of the Philadelphia Museum of Art since the 1983 College Art Association session on the painting and contributed useful insights to our research project include: J.R.J. van Asperen de Boer, James Snyder, Carlenrica Spantigati, Molly Faries, Anne van Buren, Dana Goodgal-Salem, Leslie Ann Blacksberg, John Hand, John Plummer, Henning Bock, John Walsh, Richard Judson, Evan Turner, and Charles Rhyne.

3. In July 1983, Joseph Rishel and the author examined the Turin painting out of its frame at the Galleria Sabauda, Turin, with Rosalba Tardito and then curator, Carlenrica Spantigati. On November 5, 1985, the author assisted J.R.J. van Asperen de Boer in examining the Turin painting with infrared reflectography through the kindness of Carlenrica Spantigati, then director of the Galleria Sabauda in Turin.

4. For a historical discussion of nail manufacture, see Lee H. Nelson, "Nail Chronology as an Aid to Dating Old Buildings," American Association for State and Local History Technical Leaflet 48, *History News*, vol. 24, no. 11 (November 1968); see also Maureen K. Phillips, "'Mechanic Geniuses and Duckies,' A Revision of New England's Cut Nail Chronology before 1820," *APT Bulletin* (Association for Preservation Technology), vol. 25, nos. 3–4 (1994), pp. 4–15.

The author is grateful to Charles A. Phillips, Historical/Conservation Architect, Phillips & Oppermann, P.A., Winston-Salem, North Carolina, for his observations regarding the nails visible in the X-radiograph of the panel.

5. Dr. Klein's analysis also notes that the oak tree from which the panel was cut came from the Baltic region. Trees from this area were regularly imported to Bruges to provide panels for paintings because the severe climate along the Baltic coast resulted in a short growing season. The narrower growth rings in the trees produced more stable panels that responded less to changes in relative humidity. Thus paint and ground layers could remain attached to panels more securely.

6. The identification was supported with polarized-light microscopy by John G. Delly of Walter C. McCrone Associates, Inc., Chicago, in 1983. An excerpt from his report follows: "I have examined your slide, and in my opinion the sample is parchment. The fibers have the interlocking, highly ramified characteristic of collag-derived integuments, as well as the typical undulose extinction, and even the frequently seen series of parallel, wavy ridges that resemble the ridges of a lake bottom near shore, when oriented in the extinction position. In addition, your sample has numerous highly birefringent particles that may be taken as ground substance, but I believe these are residues from the liming and chalking steps. Some lime remains amongst the fibers after the unhairing process, but following the second wash, the skins are typically dusted with a chalk, and frequently rubbed with pumice. I found no pumice in your sample." The use of chalk in medieval times to de-grease or whiten parchment or to influence its drying time is discussed by R. Reed, *Ancient Skins, Parchments, and Leathers* (London and New York, 1972), p. 147.

7. Reed, 1972, p. 130.

8. For a discussion of the preparation of parchment, see Daniel V. Thompson, *The Materials and Techniques of Medieval Painting* (New York, 1956), pp. 24–29.

9. Because the Johnson Collection painting is so small and its layers so thin, it was deemed undesirable to take samples large enough for medium analysis by more sophisticated instrumental means available at the time the painting was being examined.

10. Viewing through a low-powered stereomicroscope, minute samples were taken, by the author, from the surface of each major paint tone of the painting. The samples, as small as 25 μm (1/1000 inch), were dispersed and mounted on microscope slides and examined with transmitted, polarized light at 350 to 1,000 magnifications. These samples were used to identify pigments and estimate the proportion of each pigment within the sample. Because of the small size of the painting, only two minute cross-section samples were taken. These were from the gray rocks at the left edge at the edge of a loss. These samples were cut down through the layers of paint to the support to show the stratigraphy of the paint layers and were mounted in a plastic resin which, when solidified, could be polished for viewing in reflected light at 100 to 200 magnifications. Additional samples from the border enabled study of the stratigraphy of that element of the picture (see Appendix 1).

11. Through the kindness of Ross Merrill at the National Gallery of Art, Washington, D.C., the Philadelphia painting was examined with X-ray fluorescence on October 22, 1986, by Paul Angiolillo. The report appears in Appendix 2.

12. See Paul Coremans, *L'Agneau mystique au Laboratoire* (Antwerp, 1953), for a discussion of the multilayered stratigraphy of the paint layers in the panels of the Ghent altarpiece which are, of course, on a much larger scale than the Johnson and Turin paintings. See also Pim W.F. Brinkman et al., "Het Lam Godsretabel van Eyck: Een Heronderzoek naar de Materialen en Schildermethoden," *Bulletin of the IRPA-KIK* (Institut Royal du Patrimoine Artistique Koninklijk Instituut voor het Kunstpatrimonium), vol. 20 (1984), pp. 137–66.

13. See Rutherford J. Gettens and George L. Stout, *Painting Materials: A Short Encyclopaedia* (New York, 1966), pp. 149–51.

14. Conversations with Alexander Yow, Conservator of Manuscripts at the J. Paul Getty Museum of Art, proved very illuminating on the occasion of his examination of the Johnson Collection painting with the author on January 9, 1987, in the Philadelphia Museum of Art conservation laboratory. Mr. Yow described an example he had seen where parchment mounted on panel had split the wood of the panel, suggesting that parchment is so strong it could influence the crackle pattern even where mounted on wood.

15. Roger Fry, Editorial Letter, *The Burlington Magazine*, vol. 48 (1926), p. 274.

16. See Gettens and Stout, 1966, pp. 173–74.

17. Through the kindness of Maryan Ainsworth, Senior Research Fellow, Paintings Conservation, The Metropolitan Museum of Art, New York, the author was able to study the *Head of Christ* attributed to Petrus Christus (c. 1445, oil on parchment on wood, 5¾ x 4⅛" [14.6 x 10.4 cm], 60.71.1), using a low-powered stereomicroscope. Similar in size to the Johnson painting, it also has a single base layer of paint upon which details have been added for the hair, blood, and so forth. It, too, has an irregular net crackle, suggesting that the paint layers responded to the expansion and contraction of the parchment rather than to the panel. Likewise, this painting has a border painted around the edge of the parchment: a black shadow line down the left side and a white line across the bottom, providing a three-dimensional effect similar to the border on the Johnson painting.

18. The Johnson Collection file for *Saint Francis Receiving the Stigmata* (cat. 314) contains a letter dated August 8, 1949, from Paul Coremans, then director of the Laboratoire Central des Musées de Belgique, to David Rosen, restorer at the Walters Art Gallery, Baltimore, who often treated Johnson pictures. Mr. Coremans asked for a photograph and an X-radiograph of the *Saint Francis* to take with him on September 10, 1949, to Turin, where he planned to photograph and sample the Turin *Saint Francis*. In November 1988, Liliane Masschelein-Kleiner, director of the Institut Royal du Patrimoine Artistique, very kindly arranged to have the Coremans samples from the Turin painting reviewed again. Leopold Kockaert's report of November 29, 1988, stated that most of the ten samples had deteriorated beyond use but it was possible to remount and analyze three cross sections by microchemical examination.

19. J.R.J. van Asperen de Boer, personal communication with the author.

20. See "Some Technical Observations on the Turin and Philadelphia Versions of 'Saint Francis Receiving the Stigmata'" by J.R.J. van Asperen de Boer in this volume, which discusses the Eyckian underdrawing in the Turin picture. See also J.R.J. van Asperen de Boer, "A Scientific Re-examination of the Ghent Altarpiece," *Oud Holland*, vol. 93, no. 3 (1979), pp. 141–214, for a detailed discussion of the underdrawing of the altarpiece and of the special characteristics of Eyckian underdrawing. Photomicrographs of cross sections taken from the paint layers of the altarpiece illustrate the multilayered complexity of the paint stratigraphy of the large-scale paintings of the altarpiece.

21. Recent contributions that help to illuminate aspects of workshop practice in the fifteenth century in Flanders include the following: Jeltje Dijkstra, *Origineel en Kopie, Een onderzoek naar de navolging van de Meester van Flémalle en Rogier van der Weyden* (Amsterdam, 1990); Lorne Campbell, "The Early Netherlandish Painters and Their Workshops," in *Le Dessin sous-jacent dans la peinture. Colloque III, 1979*, ed. D. Hollanders-Favart and Roger Van Schoute (Louvain-la-Neuve, 1981), pp. 43–61; Jean C. Wilson, "Workshop Patterns and the Production of Paintings in Sixteenth-Century Bruges," *The Burlington Magazine*, vol. 132 (1990), pp. 523–27; Jean C. Wilson, "Connoisseurship and Copies: The Case of the Rouen Grouping," *Gazette des Beaux-Arts*, 6th period, vol. 117 (May–June 1991), pp. 191–206.

The author is grateful to Leslie Ann Blacksberg for having brought these articles to her attention and to Dana Goodgal-Salem for having shared information about relationships within Jan van Eyck's workshop, and especially to Anne van Buren who, in her February 1991 talk "The Afterlife of Some Eyckian Patterns," at the College Art Association session at the National Gallery of Art, Washington, D.C., and on her visit in June 1991 to study the Johnson picture in the laboratory, further illuminated the investigation of relationships within Jan van Eyck's workshop resulting from her own research into the Turin-Milan Hours and related subjects.

22. Molly Faries carried out an extensive infrared reflectography analysis of *The Annunciation* in 1981 and found Eyckian underdrawing throughout the painting. She reported her findings in her talk "The Underdrawing of *The Annunciation* and the Question of Eyckian Style," at the

February 1991 College Art Association meeting at the National Gallery of Art, Washington, D.C., which explored this painting.

23. David Bull, Chairman of Painting Conservation at the National Gallery of Art, Washington, D.C., very kindly arranged for the author to examine *The Annunciation* with a stereomicroscope in the laboratory on April 3, 1992. At that time Mr. Bull had completed the removal of discolored surface coatings and retouchings and had not yet begun inpainting. This provided an unusual opportunity to study the brushwork fully revealed. Following this cleaning, Melanie Gifford, Research Conservator for Painting Technology at the National Gallery, carried out an extensive technical study of *The Annunciation*; see Gifford, "Jan van Eyck's *Annunciation*: Development and Alterations," in *Le Dessin sous-jacent dans la peinture. Colloque X, 1993: Le Dessin sous-jacent dans le processus de création*, ed. Hélène Verougstraete and Roger Van Schoute (Louvain-la-Neuve, 1995), pp. 81–93.

24. J.R.J. van Asperen de Boer, Bernhard Ridderbos, and Manja Zeldenrust, "'Portrait of a Man with a Ring' by Jan van Eyck," *Bulletin van het Rijksmuseum* (special issue), vol. 39 (1991), pp. 8–35.

25. The Turin-Milan Hours manuscript was examined with infrared reflectography by J.R.J. van Asperen de Boer and the author on November 6 and 7, 1985, through the kindness of Silvana Pettenati, director of the Museo Civico d'Arte Antica in Turin. The results were published by Marigene H. Butler and J.R.J. van Asperen de Boer, "The Examination of the Milan-Turin Hours with Infrared Reflectography: A Preliminary Report," in *Le Dessin sous-jacent dans la peinture. Colloque VII, 1987*, ed. Roger Van Schoute and Hélène Verougstraete-Marcq (Louvain-la-Neuve, 1989), pp. 71–76.

26. See the excerpt from the will of Anselme Adornes, filed 1470, in C. Aru and E. de Geradon, *La Galerie Sabauda de Turin*, vol. 5 of *Les Primitifs flamands: 1. Corpus de la peinture des anciens Pays-Bas méridionaux au quinzième siècle* (Antwerp, 1952), p. 13, pl. XIX (see fig. 6).

Peter Klein

Dendrochronological Analyses of the Two Panels of "Saint Francis Receiving the Stigmata"

The aim of dendrochronological analysis is to give a terminus post quem for the component boards of paintings on panel by providing an exact dating for the youngest measured growth ring of the wood. Furthermore, a comparison of the growth ring series of different boards can show whether or not they originated from the same tree, and consequently sometimes permits an attribution to a particular workshop.[1] In deriving the felling date of a tree used for panels, a statistically probable allowance for the sapwood (usually removed) and an average length of seasoning time must be considered.

Oak panels were usually cut from the tree trunk with an approximately radial orientation and therefore contain a large number of growth rings. In most cases, Netherlandish pictures are painted on oak panels of Polish/Baltic origin, as has recently been determined.[2] The outer portion of sapwood is light colored and perishable; it was usually trimmed away by the panelmaker. The allowance for sapwood growth rings is a statistical average, whereby 15 years is the median, and 50 percent of the number of sapwood rings lie between 13 and 19 years. The lower and upper extreme values are 9 and 36 years.

Determination of the felling date for panels that are dated also provides information on the amount of time wood was customarily stored before being used for a painting. The investigations carried out with signed and dated Netherlandish panels of the fifteenth century indicate a usual seasoning time of 10 to 15 years.[3]

Normally the measurements for a dendrochronological analysis are taken from panels whose edges permit a clear reading of the growth rings. In the case of the Philadelphia panel of *Saint Francis Receiving the Stigmata*, the measurements could only be taken from an X-radiograph. Measurements on the X-radiograph showing the wood structure in the radial direction resulted in a mean curve with 83 growth rings. By comparison with the master chart of the Baltic/Polish region, the growth rings can be dated between 1225 and 1307.

From further comparisons evaluating the ring curves of different paintings by Jan van Eyck, it is evident that the growth ring curve of the panel supporting the Philadelphia *Saint Francis* is identical with the last part of the growth ring curve from the wood used for the Van Eyck panels *Portrait of Giovanni Arnolfini* (fig. 59) and *Portrait of Baudouin de Lannoy* (fig.

60). Figure 61 shows the probable juxtaposition of the three panels superimposed on a tree cross section. The 177 growth rings from the *Arnolfini* panel can be dated between 1206 and 1382, and the 179 growth rings from the *Baudouin* panel between 1205 and 1383 (fig. 62). The youngest measured heartwood ring of all the panels from the same tree grew in the year 1383.

In terms of the sapwood statistics for Eastern Europe, an earliest felling date for the year 1392 can be derived. Under statistical view, a felling date is most plausible between 1396 . . . 1398 . . . 1402+x. Assuming the median of 15 sapwood rings and 10 years' storage time, the creation of these three paintings would have been possible from 1408 upward.

In addition to the panel of the Philadelphia *Saint Francis*, the panel of the Turin *Saint Francis* was analyzed. This oak panel consists of two boards vertically glued together. On board I (the left side in a frontal view), 87 growth rings could be measured, and on the right side, board II has 84 rings. The two boards originated from the same tree. Consulting the master chart of the Baltic/Polish region, board I can be dated between 1273 and 1359, and board II between 1282 and 1365. The youngest heartwood ring grew in the year 1365.

A determination of the original between the two panels in Philadelphia and Turin cannot be derived by dendrochronological analysis alone. However, it is obvious that the wood for the *Saint Francis* in Philadelphia originated from the same tree as two other panels by Jan van Eyck, the portraits of Baudouin de Lannoy and Giovanni Arnolfini, both in the Gemäldegalerie, Staatliche Museen zu Berlin Preussischer Kulturbesitz, Berlin.

Fig. 61. Juxtaposition of three Van Eyck panels, cut radially from the same tree: the Philadelphia *Saint Francis*, *Portrait of Baudouin de Lannoy*, and *Portrait of Giovanni Arnolfini*.

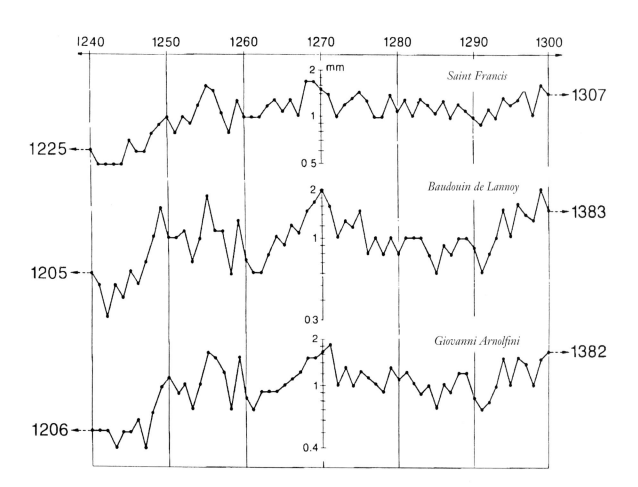

Fig. 62. Comparison of tree growth-ring sequences of the Philadelphia *Saint Francis*, *Portrait of Baudouin de Lannoy*, and *Portrait of Giovanni Arnolfini*.

NOTES

1. Peter Klein, "The Differentiation of Originals and Copies of Netherlandish Panel Paintings by Dendrochronology," in *Le Dessin sous-jacent dans la peinture. Colloque VII, 1989*, ed. Hélène Verougstraete-Marcq and Roger Van Schoute (Louvain-la-Neuve, 1991), pp. 29–42.

2. D. Eckstein, T. Wazny, J. Bauch, and P. Klein, "New Evidence for the Dendrochronological Dating of Netherlandish Paintings," *Nature*, vol. 320 (1986), pp. 465–66.

3. Peter Klein, "Dendrochronological Studies on Oak Panels of Rogier van der Weyden," in *Le Dessin sous-jacent dans la peinture. Colloque VII, 1987*, ed. Roger Van Schoute and Hélène Verougstraete-Marcq (Louvain-la-Neuve, 1989), pp. 25–36.

J.R.J. van Asperen de Boer

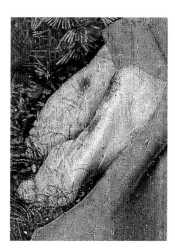

Some Technical Observations on the Turin and Philadelphia Versions of "Saint Francis Receiving the Stigmata"

The panel painting *Saint Francis Receiving the Stigmata* now in the Galleria Sabauda in Turin (pl. II)[1] is first recorded at the beginning of the nineteenth century; it was sold in 1866 to the Royal Gallery in Turin.[2] The same subject is depicted in a smaller painting purchased by John G. Johnson in 1894, and now housed at the Philadelphia Museum of Art (pl. I). Previously, the Philadelphia picture had been sold in Lisbon between 1824 and 1827, when it arrived in London.[3]

In 1857 G. F. Waagen published it as by Jan van Eyck.[4] In 1886 W. H. James Weale identified the two pictures with those mentioned in the will of Anselme Adornes, dated February 10, 1470.[5] The original of this will is lost, but in 1860 Alexandre Pinchart published a transcript dating from the early sixteenth century, then preserved at the Stadsarchief in Bruges.[6] A photograph of this document was published in 1952 by C. Aru and E. de Geradon in the Turin Corpus of *Les Primitifs flamands* with a transcription of the Flemish text (fig. 6).[7] The will states: "item zo gheve ic elcken van myne lieve dochters . . . een tavereel daerinne dat sinte Franciscus in potrature van meester Jans handt van Heyck ghemaect staet" (Item, I give to each of my dear daughters . . . a picture wherein Saint Francis in portraiture from the hand of Master Jan van Eyck). This has led many authors to accept both paintings as originals by Jan van Eyck.

Others have recognized in the Turin version a copy made by a painter of the next generation,[8] and in 1935 G. J. Hoogewerff proposed Petrus Christus.[9] It has been pointed out that if the identification of the two panels with the *tavereelkins* mentioned in the will of Anselme Adornes is correct, Anselme could not have received both panels directly from Jan van Eyck, as he would have been only seventeen years old when the painter died in 1441.[10] Indeed, it would have been pointless at that age for him to purchase two versions of the same subject for as yet unborn children. It is certainly more plausible to assume that one was copied after the other when a "souvenir" was wanted for each of two Adornes daughters.

In view of the existing data on Eyckian underdrawing,[11] it seemed feasible to determine whether both pictures would or would not fit into the Eyckian group from that point of view. A first rapid scanning of the Philadelphia painting with infrared reflectography in September

1981 by the author did not show underdrawing. Marigene Butler examined the picture again with the infrared reflectography equipment of the Philadelphia Museum of Art in 1985 and was able to show sets of parallel strokes in the right cuff of Saint Francis.[12] Following a suggestion by the author to Marigene Butler in 1984, the Turin picture was examined with infrared reflectography in November 1985 due to the most amiable courtesy of Carlenrica Spantigati, then director of the Galleria Sabauda (fig. 63).[13]

Certainly there was a point in assessing whether the Turin picture could be Eyckian or not, because there is evidence that different versions of the same picture were made in the Netherlands from the middle of the fifteenth century onward. A notable example is provided by the copies of the *Notre-Dame de Grâce*, brought from Rome to Cambrai, of which Petrus Christus made three copies for the Count d'Estampes in 1454 and Hayne de Bruxelles, twelve, in 1454–55.[14] None of the Petrus Christus copies have survived, but two identical versions of a *Madonna and Child* attributed to Petrus Christus are extant: one of these is in the Budapest Museum of Fine Arts, the other in the Museum Boymans–van Beuningen, Rotterdam.[15]

Examination of paintings in the Petrus Christus group with infrared reflectography had made it clear already in 1985 that the style of their underdrawing is sufficiently distinctive from that in the Van Eyck group.[16] Thus, were the Turin picture to show underdrawing, it could be assumed a priori that a stylistic assignment of its authorship was feasible. Examination of the Turin painting with infrared reflectography showed, indeed, that it is fully underdrawn in a style quite compatible with Eyckian underdrawing.[17]

Description of the Underdrawing in the Turin Painting

The robe of Saint Francis is underdrawn in detail (figs. 64, 65). The main folds are first indicated by lines showing up somewhat lighter than the ultimate shadows; slight shifts in contours are thus produced. Zones of shadow are prepared in the underdrawing by several types of hatching. In the sleeves, on the front of the habit near the knees, and in the folds below the waist, hatchings run parallel to the main contour. In the lower part of Saint Francis's robe, in the sleeves, and near the neck, convex folds are shaded by a series of short, parallel strokes perpendicular to the main fold. On the sleeves this type of hatching seems to be superimposed upon a system of longer shading hatchings. Modeling is also emphasized by hatchings on the breast of the saint.

The habit of the sitting friar shows much the same approach in its underdrawing. There are perhaps more slightly curved, parallel hatchings perpendicular to the fold in preparing rounded surfaces. Modifications from the underdrawn folds and contours have occurred during painting, notably near the foot at the right. The lowest contour of the habit is also crenated in the underdrawing, albeit on different parts of the rim. In the reflectograms of the friar's habit, the darkest fold lines seem to be clearly defined in the underdrawing as well; they sometimes end in short hooks and are not always followed during painting.

The face of each friar looks different in the reflectograms. In the underdrawing Saint Francis's face is more turned away from the spectator and tilted further upward—as can be seen from the position of the ear and the line of the chin revealed in the reflectograms (figs. 66, 67). The hood lay farther from the neck. Saint Francis's right eye was first lower; the painted iris and pupil are also visible in the reflectograms. The hair seen in the reflectograms as a few thickish brush strokes leaves no doubt about the intended tonsure. Before the restoration in 1982 this was

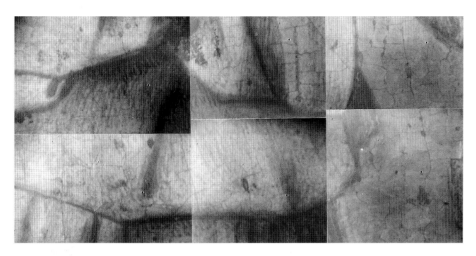

Fig. 64. Infrared reflec-
togram assembly of a detail
of the robe of Saint Francis
in the Turin *Saint Francis*.

Fig. 65. Detail of the robe
of Saint Francis in the
Turin *Saint Francis*.

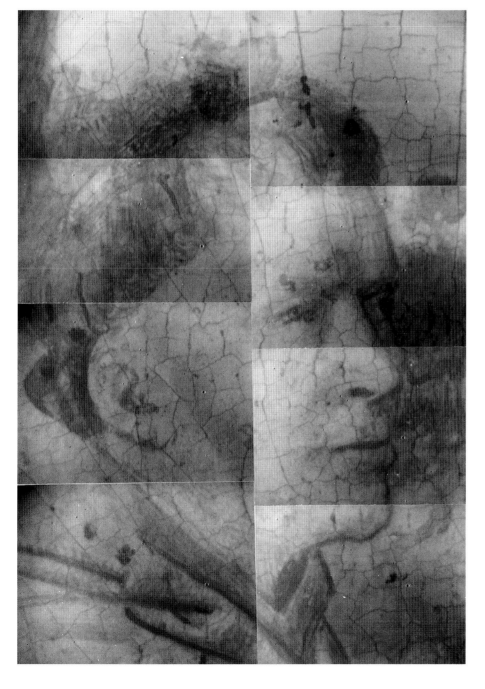

Fig. 67. Detail of the face
of Saint Francis in the
Turin *Saint Francis*.

Fig. 66. Infrared reflec-
togram assembly of the
face of Saint Francis in the
Turin *Saint Francis*.

also visible on the painting, but it is less obvious now, as the present appearance of the top of the head is a little confusing. Some shading on the forehead, beneath the chin, and perhaps on the cheeks is visible in the reflectograms. At the right of the profile, underdrawing probably associated with the trees in the background is visible in the reflectograms. It could be taken for a first, sketchy profile, but this seems unlikely.

The face of the sitting friar is seen more *en face*, his left cheek and left eye being visible. His right hand was broader, and the reflectograms strongly suggest that his left hand was initially supposed to clamp his head as well (figs. 68, 69). This would also seem to follow from the delimitation in the overlapping hatchings indicating the friar's shadow on the rock in the underdrawing. The hands of Saint Francis show only minor shifts.

The feet of the friar are difficult to read in the reflectograms; the one at the right may have been larger, as a lower contour is visible. Near the edge of the painting the reflectograms show a ghost of a toe with perhaps a foot and a curving contour in the rock above. This may have been a first outline, with the little stream not planned. The damage of the two feet slightly below them shows up clearly in the reflectograms (figs. 70, 71). It is hardly visible in the X-radiograph.

The feet of Saint Francis, interestingly, were underdrawn not naked but with some form of footwear—perhaps a sock or a close-fitting shoe—with a rim at the ankle (figs. 72, 73). Their position was different as well, and the placement of Saint Francis's right foot and ankle as seen in the reflectograms indicates a rather more acceptable anatomical position for his knee.

Various contours for the feet of Saint Francis can be observed in the reflectograms, and, in combination with the higher density there in the X-radiograph, it can be concluded that the artist did considerable searching in this area.

The most noticeable changes in the foreground are in the rocks and stones of different sizes and in different positions revealed in the reflectograms of the lower-right corner. The one or two rocks supplanted by the painted stream are somewhat reminiscent of the ones at the right in Van Eyck's *Saint Barbara* (fig. 74).

The rock formations themselves are also underdrawn, showing more pronounced contrast in their various faces in the reflectograms. These forms were frequently modified during painting—notably at the right of the Crucifix and at the left of Saint Francis's back. Some of these changes show up in the X-radiograph, suggesting underpainting following the underdrawing.[18] The detailed underdrawing of the rocks on the horizon at the left was not always precisely followed by the artist in the painting process.

The tree in the upper-left corner was underdrawn larger, at an oblique angle, and with wintry branches (figs. 75, 76); an even nuder tree on the rock at the right of the Crucifix was not retained in painting (fig. 77).

Smaller trees are also indicated in the underdrawing. A row of trunks jotted down with a thickish brush shows at the left of Saint Francis's shoulder, and some contours of their foliage are indicated. None of the herbs or flowers is underdrawn.

The Crucifix is also underdrawn (figs. 78, 79). The city in the background has fewer windows and crenellations in the underdrawing, often in slightly different positions from the painted ones; there are some small changes such as the form of the spire of the large tower (figs. 80, 81).

It would seem that a number of characteristics can be found in the Turin underdrawing quite typical of the Eyckian style:

1. Most hatchings in the robes run parallel to the main fold or contour, but short hatchings perpendicular to the fold also occur.[19]
2. Details such as the tree in the upper-left corner, the rock in the lower-right corner, and the cross are underdrawn with some detail.
3. The city in the background is indicated in the underdrawing with windows in their approximate positions. This also occurs in the underdrawing of the left background of the *Adoration of the Lamb* panel in the Ghent altarpiece, in the *Three Marys at the Sepulchre* in Rotterdam (fig. 20), and in the Louvre *Virgin of Chancellor Rolin* (fig. 105).[20] It seems to be an Eyckian idiosyncrasy that is independent of the format of the cityscape depicted.
4. That the feet of Saint Francis were first underdrawn with some form of footwear and thus did not show the stigmata was an iconographical error, which the artist corrected during painting. Such corrections have been shown to have occurred in the genesis of the Ghent altarpiece as well and could be taken as typically Eyckian.[21]

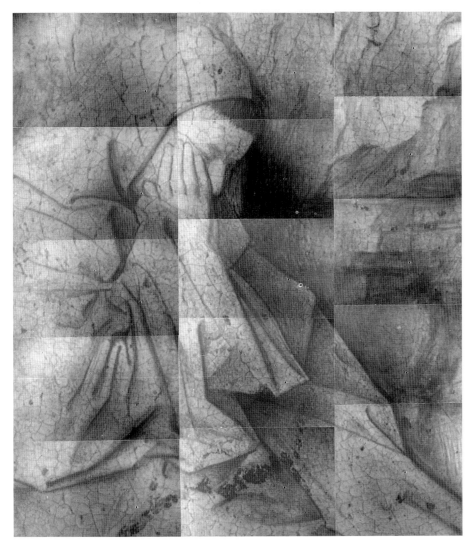

Fig. 68. Infrared reflectogram assembly of a detail of Brother Leo in the Turin *Saint Francis*, showing his left hand seeming to clamp his head.

Fig. 69. Detail of Brother Leo in the Turin *Saint Francis*.

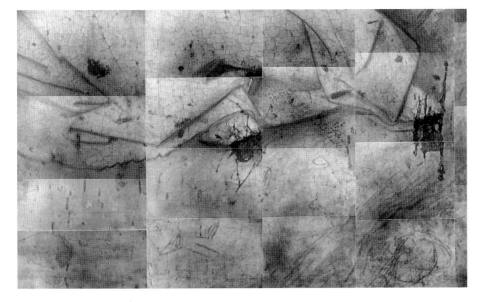

Fig. 70. Infrared reflectogram assembly of a detail showing Brother Leo's feet in the Turin *Saint Francis*. The stone was in a different position in the underdrawing.

Fig. 71. Detail of Brother Leo's feet in the Turin *Saint Francis*.

Several authors have criticized the clumsy anatomy of the feet of Saint Francis and of the friar.[22] Clearly, the disposition of both Saint Francis's feet and his hidden legs seems more satisfactorily rendered in the position revealed by infrared reflectography.

Both feet of Brother Leo have been damaged by scratches slightly below the position of the actual feet. The retouchings of these feet in the Turin painting have certainly confused the anatomy still further. In the Philadelphia version the sole of the lower foot can clearly be seen; in the Turin panel this is not very evident today. It should also be remembered, however, that even in the Ghent altarpiece anatomically strange positions occur, for instance in the hand of the Prophet Micah.[23]

As an Eyckian origin of the Turin panel can thus now be confidently assumed, the possibility that both versions are non-Eyckian later copies can be discarded, and the traditional equation to the Adornes pictures becomes more probable.

Some additional material evidence can be interpreted as favoring the identification with the *tavereelkins* mentioned in the Adornes will. The format of the Turin panel is suitable for receiving two *duerkens*, or wings, with the *personage*[s] of Adornes and his wife—they would have been about 11½ by 6½ inches (30 x 17 cm). If one assumes that *potrature* must signify a portrait such as that of Petrus Christus's *Portrait of a Carthusian*[24]—which is only 8⅛ inches wide (20.3 cm)—then it is difficult to see how a panel of such a format could receive wings. However, it seems that *potrature* was used in a fairly broad sense in the fifteenth century.

The Turin *Saint Francis* panel was probably intended as a solitary painting; its marbleized reverse (fig. 17) points to this, as it is also found on the *Virgin of Chancellor Rolin* (fig. 105) and several other Eyckian paintings. In view of its small size, it may have had an Eyckian type of frame with a painted imitation of stone. Possibly this frame was not directly suitable for receiving wings, and a pedestal to convert it into a triptych for private devotion may have been added. The panel could have been fitted into a larger frame, and the original frame removed at that point. The Turin panel has no *barbe*, or unpainted edge, but this is likely the result of a later cropping, as it has been observed that a strip of approximately 5 millimeters on the

Philadelphia painting at the left edge is now missing in the Turin picture;[25] also at the right edge more is visible in the Philadelphia version.

The fact that the Philadelphia picture is painted on parchment attached to a panel first led to an association with Eyckian illuminated manuscripts, as it could have been cut out of a manuscript and pasted onto a panel. Several arguments run counter to this interpretation, however. The first is that the Philadelphia picture has been found to be painted in an oleaginous medium.[26] The usual mediums in medieval book illumination are glair and gum arabic.[27] Such mediums have been identified by methods of analytical chemistry in samples of fifteenth-century illuminated manuscripts.[28] Furthermore, an examination of the *Très Belles Heures de Notre-Dame*—the Milan Hours in the Museo Civico, Turin—with infrared reflectography has not clarified the matter, as some of the illuminations associated with Van Eyck reveal underdrawing and others do not.[29]

It has been shown that in Flemish Primitive painting of the second half of the fifteenth century, parchment was used for painting portraits, which were later pasted onto a panel.[30] Although these examples are invariably related to donors or patrons, they show that some tradition of oil painting on parchment must have existed. Investigations have confirmed that there are other kinds of extant pictures consisting of oil paint on parchment or paper pasted onto a panel.[31] Furthermore, a number of cabinet miniatures are known in which gouache paintings on parchment are pasted onto panels.[32] Once again, these pictures do not seem to occur before the second half of the fifteenth century.

In 1987 Peter Klein was able—using an X-radiograph—to arrive at a dendrochronological date for the panel on which the Philadelphia version is pasted.[33] The dating of the available rings between 1225 and 1307 is not contradictory to its having been used before Van Eyck's death in 1441. Klein also showed that the panel in Philadelphia originated from the same tree as the wood used in two other small panels, the *Portrait of Giovanni Arnolfini* and the *Portrait of Baudouin de Lannoy*, in the Gemäldegalerie, Berlin (figs. 59, 60). There is agreement in the literature about the attribution of these paintings, both of which have lost their original frames, to Van Eyck.[34]

It could be argued theoretically that the wood of all three panels came from a panel left

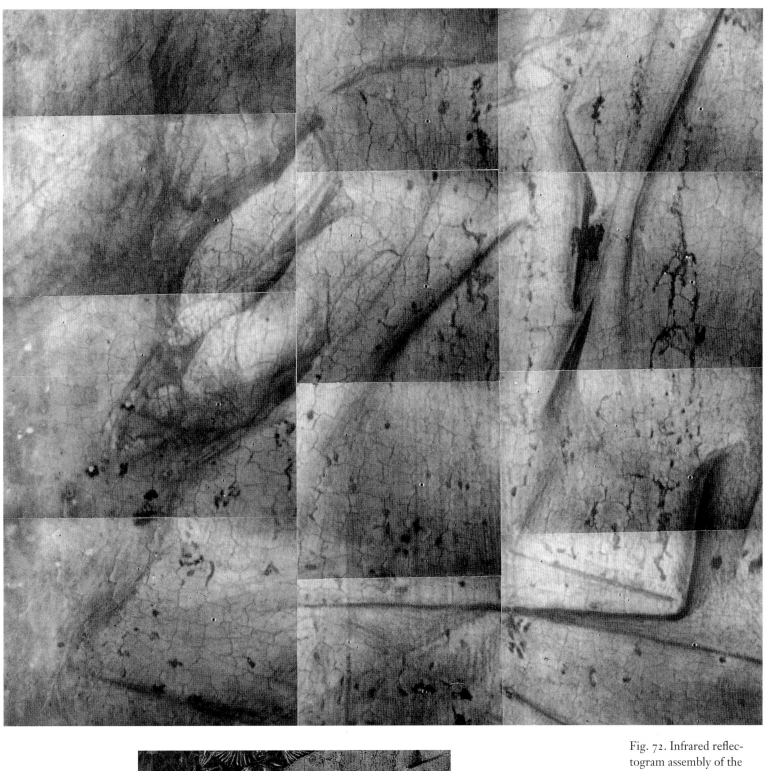

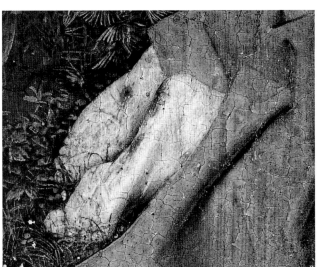

Fig. 72. Infrared reflectogram assembly of the feet of Saint Francis from the Turin *Saint Francis*. In the underdrawing, Francis's feet were covered by some form of footwear.

Fig. 73. Detail of the feet of Saint Francis from the Turin *Saint Francis*.

over from an Early Netherlandish painting or
even an Eyckian painting that was transferred or
cradled supposedly in the nineteenth century. It
is known that in 1894 a special machine was
used to saw the panels of the Ghent altarpiece,
then in Berlin.[35] Using such a thinner board, a
forger could have produced an intentional imitation or fake on an apparently Eyckian panel.
This reasoning can be refuted for the Berlin
panels; Elisabeth Dhanens not only observed
that the reverse of the Berlin Arnolfini portrait
is marbled—as is frequently the case in Eyckian
paintings—but she also discovered a fragment of
a sixteenth-century wax seal.[36]

The *Portrait of Baudouin de Lannoy* was examined in Berlin with infrared reflectography by
Marigene Butler and Gerald Schultz, the
museum's photographer, in September 1988.[37]
The underdrawing visible in a photograph of the
infrared reflectogram assembly seems stylistically
similar to the underdrawing revealed in the
Vienna *Portrait of Cardinal Albergati* and the
Bucharest *Portrait of a Man with a Ring*.[38] This

pertains to the hatching used to indicate light and
dark in the face and the broader strokes in the hat.

That the ground and the paint layers are
original to the two panels in Berlin could further
be proved by determining whether the vertical
age crackle occurs mostly at the less dense
springwood, which is darker in X-radiograph
negatives.[39] This does not apply, of course, to
the Philadelphia panel, with its pasted parchment. Considering Klein's dendrochronological
findings, there seems thus every reason to suppose that the panel in Philadelphia was at some
time in Van Eyck's studio. The painted version
of *Saint Francis Receiving the Stigmata* pasted
onto it should have been painted before Jan van
Eyck's death in 1441 to be called Eyckian. It
would then be the earliest example of an exact
copy in fifteenth-century Netherlandish painting. As all the other evidence available at present points to such copies occurring only in the
second half of the fifteenth century or later,[40]
there lingers some hesitation to admit this. The
possibility that the panel was taken over after

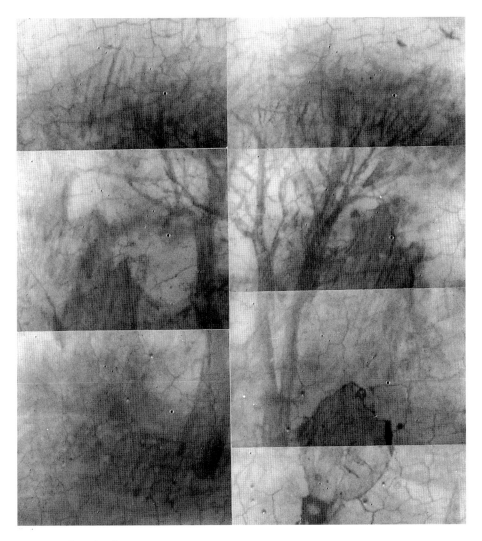

Fig. 75. Infrared reflectogram assembly of the tree in the upper left-hand corner of the Turin *Saint Francis*.

Van Eyck's death by some other painter—perhaps indeed Petrus Christus—who then copied the still-available painting now in Turin is not to be excluded. Such a post-Eyckian status would better conform with the earliest known date of 1454 for the copies of the Cambrai *Notre-Dame de Grâce* and would also accord with the influence of Eyckian heritage on illuminators from 1450 onward.[41]

In summary, the Turin picture must be considered an original by Jan van Eyck, possibly transformed into a triptych with shutters at a later date. If one accepts the association of the Turin and Philadelphia versions, it seems reasonable to suppose that the Eyckian original could have been copied on parchment at some time before 1470 to provide a second triptych for another daughter of Anselme Adornes, who was born only in 1457.[42] The possibility that such exact copies on a smaller format were already made during Jan van Eyck's lifetime cannot be ruled out, but should be investigated further.[43]

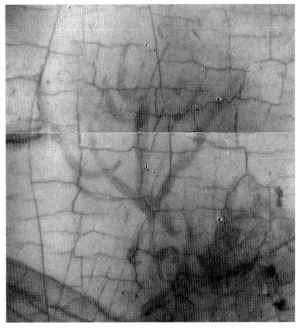

Fig. 76. Detail of the tree at the left of the Turin *Saint Francis*.

Fig. 77. Infrared reflectogram assembly of a tree on the rock at the right of the Crucifix that was not included in the final painting of the Turin *Saint Francis*.

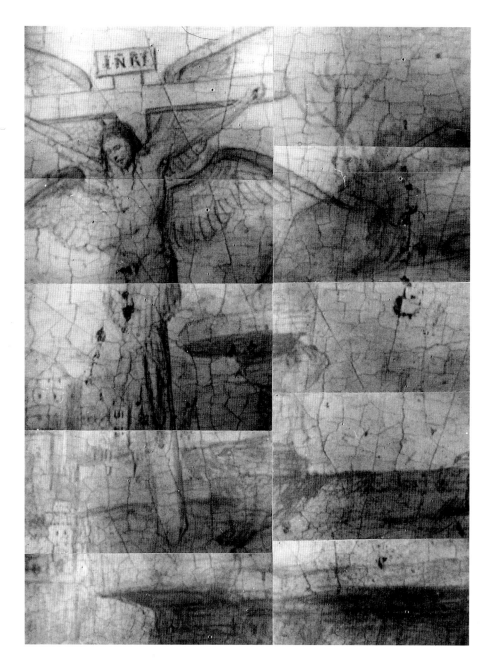

Fig. 79. Detail of the Crucifix in the Turin *Saint Francis*.

Fig. 78. Infrared reflectogram assembly of the Crucifix and the background in the Turin *Saint Francis*. The underdrawn tree was not painted out.

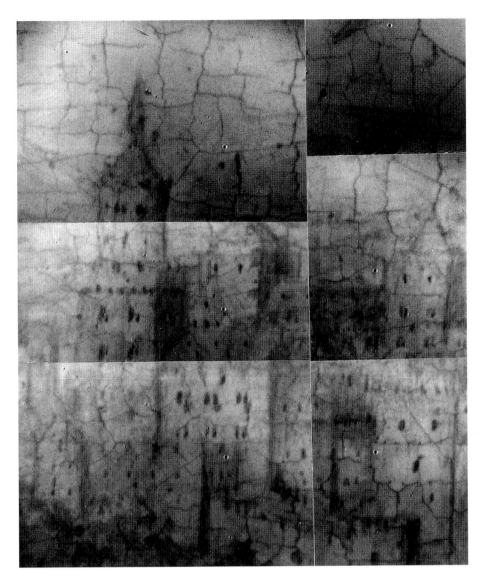

Fig. 80. Infrared reflec-
togram assembly of the
cityscape in the background
of the Turin *Saint Francis*.
The windows are under-
drawn in approximately
their intended positions.

Fig. 81. Detail of the
cityscape in the Turin
Saint Francis.

NOTES

1. The painted surface of the Turin picture measures:
11½ x 13⅛" (29.2 x 33.4 cm); the panel: 11⅝ x 13⅛"
(29.5 x 33.4 cm).

2. See C. Aru and E. de Geradon, *La Galerie Sabauda de
Turin*, vol. 5 of *Les Primitifs flamands: 1. Corpus de la peinture des anciens Pays-Bas méridionaux au quinzième siècle*
(Antwerp, 1952), pp. 5–13, esp. p. 9 with further references.

3. The painted surface of the Philadelphia picture measures: 4⅞ x 5¾" (12.4 x 14.6 cm); the panel: 6¹/₁₆ x 6⁹/₁₆"
(15.4 x 16.7 cm). [Barbara Sweeny], *John G. Johnson Collection: Catalogue of Flemish and Dutch Paintings* (Philadelphia,
1972), pp. 35–37.

4. G. F. Waagen, *Galleries and Cabinets of Art in Great
Britain. . .*, vol. 4 (supplement) of *Treasures of Art in Great
Britain, 1854–1857* (London, 1857), p. 389.

5. W. H. James Weale, "John van Eyck at the Academy
Old Masters Exhibition," *The Times* (London), February 3,
1886, p. 7.

6. Alexandre Pinchart, ed., *Archives des arts, sciences et lettres: Documents inédits* (Ghent, 1860), vol. 1, p. 267.

7. Aru and de Geradon, 1952, pl. XIX, p. 13.

8. Charles de Tolnay, *Le Maître de Flémalle et les frères
Van Eyck* (Brussels, 1939), p. 68; Ludwig Baldass, *Jan van
Eyck* (New York and London, 1952), pp. 276–77; Aru and
de Geradon, 1952, p. 8.

9. G. J. Hoogewerff, *Vlaamsche Kunst en Italiaansche
renaissance* (Antwerp, 1935), pp. 23–25.

10. See ibid.

11. J. Taubert, "Beobachtungen zum schöpferischen
Arbeitsprozess bei einigen altniederländischen Malern,"
Nederlands Kunsthistorisch Jaarboek, vol. 26 (1975), pp.
41–71; J.R.J. van Asperen de Boer, "A Scientific Re-examination of the Ghent Altarpiece," *Oud Holland*, vol. 93, no. 3
(1979), pp. 141–214.

12. See "An Investigation of the Philadelphia 'Saint
Francis Receiving the Stigmata'" by Marigene Butler in
this volume.

13. The Turin panel was examined in situ on November
5, 1985, with infrared reflectography by the author and
Marigene Butler. The author's equipment consisted of a
Grundig FA 70 television camera equipped with a Hama-
matsu N 214 infrared vidicon and provided with a Kodak
Wratten 87A cut-on filter. Both the television camera and
the Grundig BG 12 monitor were for 875 television lines.
Reflectograms were photographed from the monitor screen
with a Nikon FL2 camera with macrolens using Kodak
Panatomic-X 32 ASA black-and-white film. A positive contact print of an X-radiograph was kindly made available by

Dr. Spantigati. Father A. Dierick of Ghent provided a 1:1 color print taken before the restoration of the panel.

14. J. Dupont, "Hayne de Bruxelles et la copie de Notre-Dame de Grâces de Cambrai," *L'Amour de l'Art*, vol. 26 (1935), pp. 363–66; J. Taubert, "Zur kunstwissenschaftlichen Auswertung von naturwissenschaftlichen Gemäldeunter-suchungen," Thesis, Philipps–Universität Marburg, 1956, p. 142. See also Erwin Panofsky, *Early Netherlandish Painting: Its Origins and Character* (Cambridge, Mass., 1953), vol. 1, p. 297; C. Périer-d'Ieteren, "Une Copie de Notre-Dame de Grâce de Cambrai aux Musées royaux des Beaux-Arts de Belgique à Bruxelles," *Bulletin Koninklijke Musea voor Schone Kunsten*, nos. 3/4 (1968), pp. 111–14. For a transcription with English translations of published and unpublished documents relating to the three copies commissioned from Petrus Christus, see Maryan W. Ainsworth, with contributions by Maximiliaan P.J. Martens, *Petrus Christus: Renaissance Master of Bruges* (New York, 1994), pp. 195–96.

15. Both panels were examined for paint-layer composition by Dr. H. Kühn of Munich in 1966. The Hague version was exhibited briefly during the exhibition *Kijken en verder kijken, een nieuwe visie op twee schilderijen* at the Institute for Art History, State University of Groningen, the Netherlands, June 9–July 1, 1984. For a discussion of these two versions, see J.R.J. van Asperen de Boer, "An Identical Contemporary Version of the Petrus Christus *Madonna and Child in an Archway*," in Maryan W. Ainsworth, ed., *Petrus Christus in Renaissance Bruges: An Interdisciplinary Approach* (New York, 1995), pp. 115–21.

16. The author has examined with infrared reflectography the *Pietà* in the Musées Royaux des Beaux-Arts de Belgique, Brussels; the signed and dated *Madonna Enthroned with Saints Jerome and Francis*, in the Städelsches Kunstinstitut, Frankfurt; and the *Virgin and Child*, in the Galleria Sabauda in Turin. Molly Faries has reflectographed Petrus Christus paintings in the National Gallery of Art, Washington, D.C., and in the Nelson-Atkins Museum of Art, Kansas City, Missouri. All show underdrawing. Since then, Maryan W. Ainsworth of the Metropolitan Museum of Art, New York, has carried out a more systematic study of Petrus Christus paintings with infrared reflectography; see Ainsworth, 1994.

17. Since I submitted the first draft of this paper in 1986, Marigene Butler has reported on this examination of the Turin picture and published a number of infrared reflectogram assemblies. Marigene H. Butler, "An Investigation of Two Paintings of *The Stigmatization of Saint Francis* Thought to Have Been Painted by Jan van Eyck," in *Le Dessin sous-jacent dans la peinture. Colloque VIII, 1989*, ed. Hélène Verougstraete-Marcq and Roger Van Schoute (Louvain-la-Neuve, 1991), pp. 95–101. Dr. Peter Klein's dendrochronological dating of the Turin panel supports this; see "Dendrochronological Analyses of the Two Panels of 'Saint Francis Receiving the Stigmata'" in this volume.

18. X-radiographs of the *Three Marys at the Sepulchre* (fig. 20), in Rotterdam, also show pronounced underpainting in the rocks of the background.

19. Van Asperen de Boer, 1979, pp. 208ff.

20. The Rotterdam painting (fig. 20) was examined in 1980 by the author in collaboration with the curator J.

Giltaij and L. Blauwkuip (J.R.J. van Asperen de Boer and J. Giltaij, "Een nader onderzoek van 'De drie Maria's aan het H. Graf'—een schilderij uit de 'Groep van Eyck' in Rotterdam," *Oud Holland*, vol. 101 [1987], pp. 254–76); *The Virgin of Chancellor Rolin* was examined by the author and Molly Faries in July 1983 (J.R.J. van Asperen de Boer and Molly Faries, "La 'Vierge au Chancelier Rolin' de van Eyck: Examen au moyen de la réflectographie à l'infrarouge," *Revue du Louvre et des Musées de France*, no. 1 [1990], pp. 37–51).

21. Van Asperen de Boer, 1979, p. 204.

22. See Aru and de Geradon, 1952, p. 8.

23. See Van Asperen de Boer, 1979, fig. 11.

24. *Portrait of a Carthusian*, 1446, oil on wood, 11½ x 8⅛" (29.2 x 20.3 cm), The Metropolitan Museum of Art, New York, 49.7.19.

25. Father A. Dierick of Ghent, personal communication, January 1986.

26. See "An Investigation of the Philadelphia 'Saint Francis Receiving the Stigmata'" by Marigene Butler in this volume.

27. Daniel V. Thompson, *The Materials and Techniques of Medieval Painting* (New York, 1956), pp. 50ff.

28. Françoise Flieder, "Mise au point des techniques d'identification des pigments et des liants inclus dans la couche picturale des enluminures de manuscrits," *Studies in Conservation*, vol. 13 (1968), pp. 49–86.

29. Due to the kind courtesy of Silvana Pettenati, director of the Museo Civico d'Arte Antica in Turin, this manuscript was examined with infrared reflectography on November 6 and 7, 1985, by the author and Marigene Butler. There was no time for stereomicroscopic examination, and only a few pages could be partially scrutinized with an 8x magnifying glass. See Marigene H. Butler and J.R.J. van Asperen de Boer, "The Examination of the Milan-Turin Hours with Infrared Reflectography: A Preliminary Report," in *Le Dessin sous-jacent dans la peinture. Colloque VII, 1987*, ed. Roger Van Schoute and Hélène Verougstraete-Marcq (Louvain-la-Neuve, 1989), pp. 71–76.

30. R. H. Marijnissen and G. Van de Voorde, "Een verklarende werkwijze van de Vlaamse Primitieven. Aantekeningen bij het werk van Joos van Wassenhove, Hugo van de Goes, Rogier van der Weyden, en Hans Memlinc," *Mededelingen van de Koninklijke Akademie voor Wetenschappen, Letteren en Schone Kunsten van België. Klasse der Schone Kunsten*, vol. 44, no. 2 (1983), pp. 42–51. Tin foil, which sometimes oxidized over time, was probably also used. It has been identified by the author in pasted-in later portraits on Jan van Scorel's group portraits of *Pilgrims to Jerusalem* (Frans Halsmuseum, Haarlem, cat. 263; and Centraal Museum, Utrecht, cat. 257).

31. A good example is the *Head of Christ*, attributed to Petrus Christus, c. 1445, oil on parchment on wood, 5¾ x 4⅛" (14.6 x 10.4 cm), The Metropolitan Museum of Art, New York, 60.71.1. See Ainsworth, 1994, cat. no. 4.

32. Torben Holck Colding, *Aspects of Miniature Painting: Its Origins and Development* (Copenhagen, 1953), chap. 4.

33. See "Dendrochronological Analyses of the Two Panels of 'Saint Francis Receiving the Stigmata'" by Peter Klein in this volume.

34. See Elisabeth Dhanens, *Hubert and Jan van Eyck* (Antwerp, 1980), p. 391.

35. Paul Coremans, *L'Agneau mystique au laboratoire* (Antwerp, 1953), p. 60.

36. Dhanens, 1980, p. 336.

37. See note 26.

38. J.R.J. van Asperen de Boer, Bernhard Ridderbos, and Manja Zeldenrust, "'Portrait of a Man with a Ring' by Jan van Eyck," *Bulletin van het Rijksmuseum* (special issue), vol. 39 (1991), pp. 8–35, figs. 5, 8.

39. This is impossible to ascertain from the two photographs of X-ray negatives available to the present author.

40. Taubert (1956, p. 146) quoted from W. Schöne, *Dieric Bouts und seine Schule* (Berlin and Leipzig, 1938), p. 71: "darf doch wohl . . . festgestellt werden dasz die exakte Kopie . . . eine Schöpfung ganz eigener Art der altniederländischen Malerei ist. Ihr erstes Auftreten ist bis jetzt nicht mit Sicherheit zu bestimmen" (may, however, . . . be established that the exact copy . . . is a quite typical creation of Early Netherlandish painting. Its first appearance cannot be determined with certainty). Taubert, however, agreed with Schöne: "Es ist kein Wunder dass also erst das letzte Drittel des 15. Jahrhunderts wohl die meisten Kopien hervorgebracht hat" (It is not surprising that only the last third of the fifteenth century produced most copies; author's translation).

J. Dijkstra ("Origineel en kopie: Een onderzoek naar de navolging van de Meester van Flémalle en Rogier van der Weyden," Thesis, University of Amsterdam, 1990), has studied this aspect in detail and concludes: "It appears now that not only exact copies but the vast majority of all extant painted copies within the group Flémalle/Van der Weyden date from between 1470 and 1530" (p. 268).

41. See Maurits Smeyers, "Answering Some Questions About the Turin-Milan Hours," in *Le Dessin sous-jacent dans la peinture. Colloque VII, 1987,* ed. Roger Van Schoute and Hélène Verougstraete-Marcq (Louvain-la-Neuve, 1989), pp. 55–70, esp. p. 66.

42. The fact that a copy could be made in perfect Eyckian style about thirty years after the artist's death is now not so surprising as it might have been two decades ago. Dendrochronological examination of the Berlin *Man with the Pinks* (Staatliche Museen zu Berlin Preussischer Kulturbesitz, no. 525A), formerly attributed to Van Eyck, has shown that the panel must be later than 1468 (Peter Klein, "Dendrochronologische Untersuchungen an Gemäldetafeln," *Berliner Museen, Beiheft Forschungen,* vol. 3 [1979], pp. 6–9). Similarly, the smaller version of the Van der Weyden-group Saint John altarpiece in the Städelsches Kunstinstitut Frankfurt has been shown to be painted on panels that must postdate 1498 (Peter Klein, "Dendrochronologische Untersuchungen an Eichenholztafeln von Rogier van der Weyden," *Jahrbuch der Berliner Museen,* vol. 23 [1981], pp. 113–23). See also Peter Klein, "The Differentiation of Originals and Copies of Netherlandish Panel Paintings by Dendrochronology," in *Le Dessin sous-jacent dans la peinture. Colloque VIII, 1989,* ed. Hélène Verougstraete-Marcq and Roger Van Schoute (Louvain-la-Neuve, 1991), pp. 29–42.

43. Charles Sterling, "Jan van Eyck avant 1432," *Revue de l'Art,* no. 33 (1976), p. 33, mentions that during Van Eyck's journey to Portugal in 1428–29: "Van Eyck commença le portrait de la princesse pour le terminer le 12 février. Il le peignit en deux exemplaires, pour plus de sûreté, l'un à acheminer par voie de terre, l'autre par mer. Retenons que quatre semaines ont suffi au maître privé de toute aide de son atelier pour mener à bien deux tableaux, sans doute petits."

This is not borne out by the text of a contemporary narrative (c. 1430) of the journey to Portugal, published by W. H. James Weale, *Hubert and John van Eyck: Their Life and Work* (London and New York, 1908): "Avec ce, les dits ambaxadeurs, par ung nommé maistre Jehan de Eyk, varlet de chambre de mon dit seigneur de Bourgoingne et excellent maistre en art de painture, firent paindre bien au vif la figure de ma dite dame l'infante Elizabeth. . . . Et, ce fait, les dits ambaxadeurs, environ le xij^e de Febvrier ensuivant, envoyerent devers mon dit seigneur de Bourgoingne quatre messaiges, deux par mer et deux par terre . . . par lesquelz messaiges, et par chascun d'iceulx, ils escripsirent à mon dit seigneur de Bourgoingne ce qu'ilz avoient trouvé . . . Aussi luy envoyerent ilz la figure de la dicte dame faicte par painctre, comme dit est" (pp. lix–lx).

The author is indebted to Prof. M. Smeyers for bringing this passage to his attention.

Fig. 82. *Saint Thomas
Aquinas in His Study*,
illuminated page from the
Turin-Milan Hours,
c. 1440–45, 11 x 7⅞"
(28 x 20 cm), Biblioteca
Universitaria, Turin, MS
K.IV.29, fol. 73v (burnt in
1904).

Maurits Smeyers

The Philadelphia-Turin Paintings and the Turin-Milan Hours

In 1904, part of the Turin-Milan Hours that burned in the Biblioteca Universitaria at Turin included the prayer to Saint Thomas Aquinas, illustrated with a scene showing this saint in his study (fig. 82).[1] The face of Saint Thomas and other areas on the miniature were slightly damaged.[2] This miniature is attributed to Master I, one of the artists who contributed to this Book of Hours in the Netherlands.[3]

This miniature is clearly related to the Eyckian painting of Saint Jerome now in the Detroit Institute of Arts (fig. 83). Not only are two learned scholars shown working in their cells or studies, but the entire compositions and numerous details in both works of art are also identical. This similarity applies to the furnishings of the rooms and to the disposition of the objects, including the chair with interlacing at the back, the rear wall of the room with a bookcase that can be curtained off and in which books are piled in disorder, the astrolabe hanging on one of the shelves, and the writing table with a reading desk, hourglass, sandbox, writing materials, and a folded letter with a text. The wooden side door of the compartment underneath the writing desk in the miniature is open, unlike that in the painting of Saint Jerome, yet in both cases it is decorated with an openwork rose. Even the colors in the miniature of Saint Thomas, which were recorded by Paul Durrieu before the fire of 1904,[4] are identical to those in the painting of Saint Jerome: a blue curtain, a green tablecloth, and gray walls. Indeed, a profound similarity exists between the two works.

Although the main figure occupies the same place and is depicted in nearly the same position at his desk in each scene, we see two different saints. In the painting, Saint Jerome, represented in the red dress of a cardinal, is reading, while his attribute, the lion, lies at his feet. In the miniature, Saint Thomas wears the Dominican habit and is writing. Based on the *vita* of this saint, the artist has added a crucified Christ as well as a banderole coming from Christ's mouth with the words that, according to the legend, he would have spoken while appearing to Saint Thomas in the monastery in Naples: "Thoma, omnia bene scripsisti de me."[5]

Since most of the masters completing the Turin-Milan Hours were known to have incorporated models, especially paintings, in other miniatures,[6] we may conclude that here the artist painted the miniature based on the painting of

Fig. 83. Workshop of Jan van Eyck?, *Saint Jerome in His Study*, oil on paper on panel, 8⅟₁₆ x 5¼" (20.5 x 13.3 cm), The Detroit Institute of Arts, 1925, 25-4.

Fig. 84. *Saint Jerome in His Study*, illuminated page from a Book of Hours, c. 1440–50, 5⅝ x 4⅛" (14.3 x 10.5 cm), Walters Art Gallery, Baltimore, MS 721, fol. 277v.

the end of the nineteenth century, probably in Germany.[8] Whatever the date of the panel may be, however, even assuming that it is not original, there must have been an Eyckian painting that served as the model for this one. There is considerable evidence for this: a 1492 inventory of the collection of Lorenzo de' Medici records a small panel of a Saint Jerome in his study, with a little cupboard and a lion at his feet, painted by Master Jan of Bruges.[9] The fact that the work inspired miniatures in several Brugian Books of Hours from c. 1440 to 1450 constitutes an even more compelling argument. The resemblance of one of these miniatures, now in the Walters Art Gallery, Baltimore (fig. 84) is very close. It is significant that the illustration of this manuscript is related to the Turin-Milan Hours not only in the example of Saint Jerome but also with regard to other scenes.[10] In any case, we may conclude that the panel of Saint Jerome now in Detroit displays an Eyckian character.

As previously stated, the artist exchanged the figure of Saint Jerome for one of Saint Thomas for iconographical reasons. For a model, the illuminator used yet another work from the Van Eyck group. The Dominican saint resembles the Saint Francis in *Saint Francis Receiving the Stigmata* (both the Turin and Philadelphia versions) in a remarkable way.[11] Indeed, the heads themselves are identical. In each case the face is represented in three-quarter view, although in the codex the inclination is slightly different: in the Turin and Philadelphia paintings the saint looks straight ahead (fig. 85); in the miniature he turns his eyes to a book on his desk (fig. 86). The hair *en écuelle* with the bald spot on the forehead bears a strong likeness. What is more, the shape of the cowl and the pattern of the folds of the cloak on Saint Thomas's shoulders correspond in the smallest details.

Another salient point is that the appearance of the crucified Christ from the legendary apparition to Saint Thomas was not invented by the illuminator according to his own inspiration. On the contrary, the cross and the figure of Christ, again, are taken from the Turin and Philadelphia paintings of Saint Francis (figs. 87, 88).[12] The following similarities are especially striking: the inclination of the cross, its pointed base, the inscription at the top, the blood that drips from Christ's right foot onto the wood, and the hair that hangs in thin strands and reaches his breast. The six wings, an iconographical

Saint Jerome or its prototype, but adapted the subject to a new iconographical situation.

Yet, the attribution of the Saint Jerome panel is problematic. Formerly, it was ascribed to Jan van Eyck. The discovery of the date 1442 (a year after Jan's death) at the upper left led to further speculation. During a cleaning of the painting in 1956, conservators investigated the date and determined that it was old but perhaps not original. Some scholars thought it to be a work of Petrus Christus after a lost painting by Van Eyck; according to others, it was begun by Jan and finished by an anonymous artist or was painted by a close follower of Van Eyck.[7] This problem is compounded by the proposal made, after recent examination, that the painting is modern and could not have been executed until

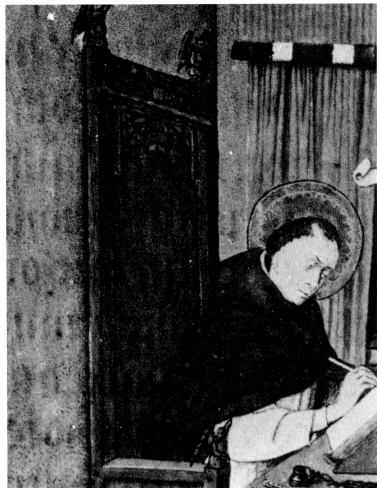

Fig. 85. Detail of the
Philadelphia *Saint Francis*.

Fig. 86. Detail of *Saint
Thomas Aquinas in His
Study* (see fig. 82).

motif that is related to the seraph-Christ appearing to Saint Francis, clearly were intentionally omitted on the miniature.

Other evidence seems to affirm that Master I, the probable illuminator of the Saint Thomas in the Turin-Milan Book of Hours, knew the *Saint Francis Receiving the Stigmata*. Buildings related to those in the background of the *Saint Francis* are found in the *bas-de-page* of the miniature from the Turin-Milan Hours showing the story of Jonah cast up by the whale (Milan part, fol. 77v),[13] and on the miniatures with the prayer of a French king (Turin part, fol. 77v), and God blessing under a canopy (Turin part, fol. 75v). One recognizes the same whiteness of the buildings, the characteristic Brugian bay, and the small paired windows, which are suggested by black dots. Equally noteworthy is a *bas-de-page* with hermits (Turin part),[14] where the figure of a seated person wrapped in a large habit with a cowl recalls, without being a copy of, Brother Leo in the Turin and Philadelphia Saint Francis paintings (fig. 89). It is interesting to note that, in depicting Saint Thomas on his deathbed in the abbey of Fossanova on the *bas-de-page* of the folio with Saint Thomas in his

study, Master I surrounded the saint with several Franciscan brothers, whose presence is not specified in his *vita*. All the miniatures used for comparison are attributed to Master I (or J), the same illuminator who, most probably, painted Saint Thomas in his study.

In the literature on Van Eyck, the attribution of the two versions of *Saint Francis Receiving the Stigmata* in Turin and Philadelphia is controversial. Here, the problem is approached from the perspective of their relationship with the Turin-Milan Hours. The attribution of the stigmatization paintings is based on the 1470 will of Anselme Adornes, which refers to two paintings by Jan van Eyck depicting Saint Francis.[15] The identification of these with the existing paintings of *Saint Francis Receiving the Stigmata* in Turin and Philadelphia is only hypothetical and, most likely, unprovable. Nonetheless, the Eyckian stylistic features of the paintings are indisputable.

Several details concerning the Eyckian context of these two versions call for special attention. The Christ figure bears a particular likeness to the one in a Calvary by Master H from the Turin-Milan Hours (fig. 90), which is a copy

Fig. 87. Detail of the Crucifix in the Philadelphia *Saint Francis*.

Fig. 88. Detail of the Crucifix in *Saint Thomas Aquinas in His Study* (see fig. 82).

Fig. 89. Detail of Brother Leo from the Philadelphia *Saint Francis*.

of a lost Eyckian panel (a later, though slightly less faithful, imitation of it is housed in the Ca' d'Oro in Venice [fig. 91]).[16] Here we see the same slender and elongated Christ, the fists clenched on the nails, and the blood flowing from the heart over the body and from the feet over the cross. The titulus, its lettering, and the abbreviations are also alike.

The radiating nimbus that appears around the head of Christ on the Calvary from Venice is not present on the figure of Christ in the earlier paintings of *Saint Francis Receiving the Stigmata* in Philadelphia and Turin, nor is it present on the Calvary scene by Master H in the Turin-Milan Hours. However, an identical nimbus does appear on the head of Christ in the Saint Thomas miniature by Master I. One assumes that it must also have existed in the prototypical Eyckian Crucifixion. The translucent *perizonium*, or loincloth, of the Christ in the Saint Thomas miniature by Master I more closely corresponds to the one on the Calvary by Master H than it does to the later painting in Venice. In terms of most details, Master H was obviously closer to the prototype than was the artist painting the later panel in Venice. From

Fig. 90. *Calvary*, illuminated page from the Turin-Milan Hours, c. 1440–45, 11 3/16 x 8" (28.4 x 20.4 cm), Museo Civico d'Arte Antica, Turin, fol. 48v.

Fig. 91. *Calvary*, after a lost work of the Van Eyck group, panel, 17¾ x 11¹³⁄₁₆" (45 x 30 cm), Galleria Giorgio Franchetti alla Ca' d'Oro, Venice.

Fig. 92. Detail of the cityscape in the Philadelphia *Saint Francis*.

this we can conclude that the master of the Saint Thomas miniature knew the Eyckian type of Christ: the source for his Christ was not the miniature by Master H, but another, now-lost Calvary, which was used also by Master H. Thus, Master I used the Crucified Christ of *Saint Francis Receiving the Stigmata*, but enriched the figure with elements of a Calvary, namely the nimbus and the body with the *perizonium*, which were also used by another illuminator of the same manuscript, Master H. That Master I employed a source other than *Saint Francis Receiving the Stigmata* is understandable, because on the stigmatization paintings the body of Christ is covered by wings.

Our attention is drawn to the city in the background of *Saint Francis Receiving the Stigmata*, which is quite rightly called an Eyckian city (fig. 92).[17] Notable is a large, white tower, flanked on the right by a lower edifice. Behind this a second large tower with an obtuse-angled roof supports a small building with a stepped gable. The same buildings are found in another painting from the Van Eyck group, namely the *Madonna with the Carthusian* in the Frick Collection in New York (fig. 93), where they are identical in color and appearance, and even in scale, to those of the larger Saint Francis painting in

Turin (fig. 94). Only the disposition of the buildings is somewhat different: in the *Madonna with the Carthusian* the stepped gable and the large tower with the pointed roof are to the left of the high tower.[18] Moreover, the mountainous background, the little boat reflected on the water, and the small figures in the landscape display similarities in the two paintings.

The *Madonna with the Carthusian* is a late work of Van Eyck, one that he most likely did not finish himself; the intervention of Petrus Christus is sometimes suggested, or, in any case, of someone from Van Eyck's atelier in the first years after his death in 1441.[19] It is worth noting that other researchers have remarked on the similarities in the rendering of the drapery of the cloaks of the Saint Francis in the stigmatization panels and the Saint Barbara in the *Madonna with the Carthusian*.[20]

The *Madonna with the Carthusian* is also related to the frontispiece of an illustrated *Cité de Dieu* made about 1445 in Bruges for Jean Chevrot, the bishop of Tournai.[21] This miniature borrows passages directly from the *Madonna with the Carthusian*, particularly in the town with the great church in the right background. The *Cité de Dieu* miniature postdates the panel, and was undoubtedly copied from it or from a common model.[22] This frontispiece returns us to the Turin-Milan Hours. In the Turin-Milan *bas-de-page* depicting the Virgins following the Lamb in a landscape (Turin part, fol. 59), one observes little hills and trees that are identical with those on the *Cité de Dieu* frontispiece. On the basis of further research on these collations, I propose that the *Cité de Dieu* frontispiece and the Turin-Milan *bas-de-page* are

not interdependent, but rather quote from one and the same Eyckian model.[23]

The following conclusions can be drawn from the above observations. The miniature with Saint Thomas in the Turin-Milan Hours quotes from two or even three different paintings from the Van Eyck group (the Saint Jerome in Detroit, the panels of *Saint Francis Receiving the Stigmata*, and a lost panel of the Calvary), and consequently is a pastiche. The *Saint Francis Receiving the Stigmata* (and by this we mean a finished panel, a model, or a drawing after the painting) was at that time known to Master I.

Moreover, most of the Eyckian works that are discussed here are related: the Saint Jerome painting now in Detroit, the *Madonna with the Carthusian* now at the Frick, and a lost panel with a Calvary. All of these paintings are related to one other in style, and they are directly connected with regard to distinct motifs. In addition, these panels can be associated with the Turin-Milan Hours, with the *Cité de Dieu* frontispiece made in Bruges for the bishop of Tournai, and with other manuscripts, such as the Book of Hours now in Baltimore. These manuscripts also display a reciprocity that reinforces

the connection with the aforementioned panels.

In this way a network of information is obtained; that which is discussed here is only a small part of the issue. In the Turin-Milan Hours, many other relationships are found with Eyckian—and even late-Eyckian or post-Eyckian—work and with other manuscripts, all of which draw upon the art of the Van Eyck group.[24] On this basis, we can establish the completion of the Turin-Milan Book of Hours to have been between 1440 and 1450 in Bruges, and, more precisely, date the intervention of Master I between 1440 and 1445. The frontispiece of the *Cité de Dieu* was painted in this workshop as well. The close relationship between the Eyckian works and the miniatures in the Turin-Milan Hours and in related manuscripts and the derivation and use of common motifs indisputably show that the illuminators used Eyckian models and were drawing upon his heritage.

The use of Eyckian models was not uncommon in this artistic milieu. From this point of view, we can confirm that there is a very close relation between the two scenes with *Saint Francis Receiving the Stigmata* in Turin and Philadelphia, and the workshop of Jan van Eyck.

NOTES

1. This part of the codex was published in 1902 by Paul Durrieu, *Heures de Turin: Quarante-cinq feuillets à peintures provenant des Très Belles Heures de Jean de France, duc de Berry* (Paris, 1902; rev. ed., Turin, 1967).

2. Paul Durrieu, "Les 'Très Belles Heures de Notre-Dame' du duc Jean de Berry. Restitution de l'état primitif d'un splendide manuscrit de XVe siècle aujourd'hui dépecé, mutilé et au tiers brûlé," *Revue Archéologique*, 4th ser., vol. 16 (1910), p. 259; and Georges Hulin de Loo, *Heures de Milan: Troisième partie des Très-Belles Heures de Notre-Dame, enluminées par les peintures de Jean de France, duc de Berry et par ceux du duc Guillaume de Bavière, comte du Hainaut et de Hollande* (Brussels and Paris, 1911), p. 48.

3. Hulin de Loo (1911, p. 48) attributed the miniature to Master K; Albert Châtelet to Master H (introduction to the revised edition of Paul Durrieu, *Heures de Turin . . .* [Turin, 1967], p. xxii); Châtelet, *Les Primitifs hollandais* (Fribourg, 1980), p. 199; and Châtelet, *Jean van Eyck, enlumineur: Les "Heures de Turin" et de "Milan-Turin"* (Strasbourg, 1993), p. 111; E. König and G. Bartz attribute the illumination to Master J ("Die erhaltenen Blätter und der verbrannte Kodex," in *Die Blätter im Louvre und das verlorene Turiner Gebetbuch* [Lucerne, 1994], p. 48). See Maurits Smeyers, "Answering Some Questions About the Turin-Milan Hours," in *Le Dessin sous-jacent dans la peinture: Géographie et chronologie du dessin sous-jacent. Colloque VII, 1987*, ed. Roger Van Schoute and Hélène Verougstraete-Marcq (Louvain-la-Neuve, 1989), pp. 55–70. See also Anne Hagopian van Buren, James H. Marrow, and Silvana Pettenati, *Heures de Turin-Milan: Inv. No. 47, Museo Civico d'Arte Antica, Torino* (Lucerne, 1996).

4. See Durrieu, 1902, p. 110, no. 41.

5. See Guilielmus de Thoco, "Vita," in J. Bollandus and G. Henschenius, eds., *Acta sanctorum*, March 1, 1865 (Paris and Rome, 1865), p. 669.

6. Smeyers, 1989, pp. 62–65.

7. See Stedelijk Museum van Schone Kunsten, Bruges, *De Eeuw der Vlaamse Primitieven* (Bruges, 1960), pp. 41–45, no. 3; The Detroit Institute of Arts and the City of Bruges, *Flanders in the Fifteenth Century: Art and Civilization. Catalogue of the Exhibition, Masterpieces of Flemish Art: Van Eyck to Bosch* (Detroit, 1960), pp. 69–72, no. 5: Giorgio T. Faggin, *L'opera completa dei van Eyck* (Milan, 1968), pp. 98–99, no. 33. The attribution to Jan van Eyck was resumed by Edwin C. Hall ("Cardinal Albergati, St. Jerome and the Detroit Van Eyck," *The Art Quarterly*, vol. 31, no. 1 [1968], pp. 3–34); and Hall, "More About the Detroit Van Eyck: The Astrolabe, the Congress of Arras and Cardinal Albergati," *The Art Quarterly*, vol. 34, no. 2 (1971), pp. 181–201; this author relates the work to Cardinal Albergati and the Congress of Arras in 1435. See Erwin Panofsky, "A Letter to Saint Jerome: A Note on the Relationship Between Petrus Christus and Jan van Eyck," in D. Miner, ed., *Studies in Art and Literature for Belle da Costa Greene* (Princeton, 1954), pp. 106–7. They are followed in this by Charles Sterling, "Jan van Eyck avant 1432," *Revue de l'Art*, no. 33 (1976), p. 56. Albert Châtelet ("Un collaborateur de Van Eyck en Italie," in Institut historique belge de Rome, *Relations artistiques entre les Pays-Bas et L'Italie à la Renaissance: Études dédiées à Suzanne Sulzberger* [Brussels and Rome, 1980], pp. 58–59), is of the opinion that the scene was painted by Master H of the Turin-Milan Hours, in Italy in 1442. This opinion is questionable and unproved. See also J. P. Howell, *Jan van Eyck and St. Jerome: A Study of Eyckian Influence on Colantonio and Antonello da Messina in Quattrocento Naples*, Ph.D. diss., University of Pennsylvania, 1976 (Ann Arbor, Mi., 1981), pp. 34–36; and Maryan W. Ainsworth, with contributions by Maximiliaan P.J. Martens, *Petrus Christus: Renaissance Master of Bruges* (New York, 1994), pp. 68–71, no. 1.

8. Roger H. Marijnissen, "On Scholarship: Some Reflections on the Study of Early Netherlandish Painting," *Mededelingen van de Koninklijke Academie voor Wetenschappen, Letteren en Schone Kunsten van België, Klasse der Schone Kunsten*, vol. 40, no. 4 (1978), pp. 1–11. Contested by Châtelet, 1980, p. 58, n. 36.

9. The text of the inventory is published in E. Müntz, *Les Collections des Médicis au XVe siècle: Le Musée-la bibliothèque-le mobilier* (Paris and London, 1888), p. 78; and in Ludwig Baldass, *Jan van Eyck* (New York and London, 1952), p. 276. In this context it may be noted that a fresco of Saint Jerome in his study by Ghirlandaio in the church of the Ognissanti in Florence shows analogies with the panel from Detroit. When the Detroit panel was acquired from private owners in 1945, family tradition held that it had been found in Italy (E. P. Richardson, "The Detroit 'St. Jerome' by Jan van Eyck," *The Art Quarterly*, vol. 19, no. 3 [1956], p. 227); these are some of the reasons why it was identified with the work in the Medici collection.

10. Maurits Smeyers, "A Mid-Fifteenth Century Book of Hours from Bruges in The Walters Art Gallery (MS 721) and Its Relation to the Turin-Milan Hours," *The Walters Art Gallery Journal*, vol. 46 (1988), pp. 69–70.

11. This was already observed by James Marrow in a review of the revised edition of Paul Durrieu, *Heures de Turin. . .* (Turin, 1967), with an introduction by Albert Châtelet, in *The Art Bulletin*, vol. 50 (1968), p. 206.

12. See also W. Bornheim, *Zur Entwicklung der Innenraumdarstellung in der niederländischen Malerei bis Jan van Eyck* (Cologne, 1940), p. 58; and F. Gorissen, *Das Stundenbuch der Katharina von Kleve: Analyse und Kommentar* (Berlin, 1973), pp. 925 and 1014ff.

13. This part is now in the Museo Civico d'Arte Antica, Turin.

14. Detached leaf in the Musée du Louvre, Paris, Cabinet des dessins, R.F. 2024.

15. Text collated by Philips Cools and published by A. De Poorter, "Testament van Anselmus Adornes, 10 Febr. 1470," *Biekorf* (Bruges), vol. 37 (1931), p. 234.

16. See Baldass, 1952, p. 282, no. 34; Faggin, 1968, p. 89, no. 8. Concerning the relation with the Turin-Milan Hours, see Smeyers, 1989, p. 63. There is also a relation to the Christ in *The Crucifixion* in the Staatliche Museen zu Berlin Preussischer Kulturbesitz, but there the hands are curved differently.

17. Erwin Panofsky, *Early Netherlandish Painting: Its Origins and Character* (Cambridge, Mass., 1953), vol. 1, p. 192, n. 1: "The landscape is a conglomeration of Eyckian motifs"; C. Aru and E. de Geradon, *La Galerie Sabauda de Turin*, vol. 5 of *Les Primitifs flamands: 1. Corpus de la peinture des anciens Pays-Bas méridionaux au quinzième siècle* (Antwerp, 1952), p. 11: "On y reconnaît tout au plus une cité eyckienne."

18. First observed in Maurits Smeyers, "Het Turijns-Milanees getijdenboek. Een bijdrage tot de Van Eyck-studie," Ph.D. diss., Louvain University, 1970, p. 748.

19. See H.J.J. Scholtens, "Jan van Eyck's 'H. Maagd met den Kartuizer' en de Exeter-Madonna te Berlijn," *Oud Holland*, vol. 55 (1938), pp. 49–62; Max J. Friedländer, *The Van Eycks—Petrus Christus*, vol. 1 of *Early Netherlandish Painting* (Leiden and Brussels, 1967), pp. 61–62; Panofsky, 1953, vol. 1, pp. 187–88; Baldass, 1952, p. 280, no. 18; Faggin, 1968, p. 98, no. 32; *The Frick Collection. Guide, the Galleries* (New York, 1979), p. 78. Josua Bruyn (*Van Eyck Problemen: De Levensbron, het werk van een leerling van Jan van Eyck* [Utrecht, 1957], pp. 20–23), mentions in this respect the author of the Fountain of Life from the Prado at Madrid. Sterling (1976, pp. 64–66), attributes the completion to Master H of the Turin-Milan Hours, working in 1433–34, thus confirming that a follower of Jan van Eyck was involved. See also Ainsworth, 1994, pp. 72–78, no. 2.

20. Hulin de Loo, 1911, p. 111; Friedländer, 1967, vol. 1, p. 63.

21. Koninklijke Bibliotheek, Brussels, MS 9015-16, fol. 1. L. Fourez, "L'Évêque Chevrot de Tournai et sa Cité de Dieu," *Revue Belge d'Archéologie et d'Histoire de l'Art*, vol. 23 (1954), pp. 73–110; G. Dogaer and M. Debae, *De librye van Filis de Goede* (Brussels, 1967), pp. 27–28, no. 24.

22. Smeyers, 1989, p. 62.

23. Smeyers, 1989, p. 62. On the miniature with God blessing (Turin part, fol. 75v), painted by Hand I, a little flowering tree is found that also occurs in the landscape on the *bas-de-page* with the Virgins and on the frontispiece of the Brugian *Cité de Dieu*.

24. See Smeyers, 1989, pp. 66–67. Among other related manuscripts are the Llangattock Hours (The J. Paul Getty Museum, Los Angeles, MS IX.7); see A. von Euw and J. M. Plotzek, *Die Handschriften der Sammlung Ludwig* (Cologne, 1982), pp. 115–41.

James Snyder

Observations on the
Iconography of Jan van Eyck's
"Saint Francis Receiving the
Stigmata"

The attribution of the *Saint Francis Receiving the Stigmata* in the John G. Johnson Collection at the Philadelphia Museum of Art (pl. I) to Jan van Eyck has been an issue of some bafflement for many years. The controversies concern its provenance, its relationship to the counterpart in Turin, and its style and position in Van Eyck's oeuvre.[1] More recently, its iconography, which has been considered sorely insipid by a number of scholars, has been questioned as worthy of the master from Bruges. Erwin Panofsky wrote that "there is no psychological relationship between the praying St. Francis and the apparition of the crucified Christ," and noted further that "the landscape is a conglomeration of Eyckian motifs rather than an integrated whole."[2] Following the censure of Panofsky, Charles Cuttler has written that "two copies of the *Stigmatization of St. Francis* are known, one in Philadelphia, the other in Turin; both show St. Francis completely disregarding the vision."[3] In his excellent catalogue of Van Eyck's works, Giorgio Faggin states that "St. Francis seems to be quite unmoved by the apparition: indeed, he does not seem to see it."[4] I would like to address these criticisms and demonstrate that the manner in which the stigmatization is experienced by Francis in the Philadelphia and Turin paintings is wholly in keeping with Van Eyck's method of representing mystical, visionary experiences and that the unusual setting is, indeed, no simple pastiche of Eyckian motifs.

Let us first review the story of the stigmatization. More has been written about Saint Francis and more images have been created of the beloved mystic from Assisi than of any other Italian saint. Born in c. 1181 at Assisi, he was the son of a wealthy merchant. His dramatic conversion to a life of poverty took place in 1203, after which he gathered about him a small band of twelve "disciples." The rule for his new Order of the Friars Minor (*Frates Minore*) was approved by Pope Innocent III in 1210. Francis received the stigmata on La Verna in 1224; he died in 1226 and was canonized in 1228. His following was immediate and widespread in Italy, and within a few decades Franciscan friars had established colonies in Spain, the south of France, Paris, and Germany. Even before his death, small Franciscan communities were reported in Flanders at Ghent and Bruges (where a convent school was purportedly founded by 1240). In 1252 a very devout lady

named Ermentrude returned from a sojourn in
Italy and converted her old anchorage in Bruges
into a convent of Clarisses, which attracted a
number of young women.[5]

    There are several reasons for the rapid
spread of the Franciscans. For one thing, Francis was a true prophet of that movement loosely
referred to as "mysticism," which swept through
Europe during the course of the fourteenth century, particularly in the north, a movement that
in time came to challenge the powerful author-
ity of the Dominican order in matters of devotion. As an exemplary mystic, Francis longed for
the direct experience of "living in and with
Christ" rather than the attainment of knowledge
of the learned proofs of orthodoxy as proposed
by the scholastics; and experience, rather than
understanding, has always been a major tenet of
mysticism. Francis read only the Gospels. He
dedicated himself to the simple and humble
vocations of Christ and the apostles, and his
touching imitation of the life of Christ, as
related by his biographers, imbued his whole
person with a boundless energy for fellowship,
love, and devotion to the poor and the meek. It
is no wonder, then, that Franciscan influence
was widespread in the Lower Rhine and the
Netherlands, where the same manner of
expressing compassion for the humble was

preached and promoted by the Brethren of the
Common Life, founded by Geert de Groote in
Deventer in the late fourteenth century, and by
later followers of the *devotio moderna*, such as
Thomas à Kempis, whose treatise the *Imitatio
Christi* (c. 1426) is still read as a guide to positive
mysticism. Hendrik Herp, a member of the
Brethren of the Common Life at Gouda and
Delft, traveled to Rome in 1450 and joined the
Franciscan order there. He returned to Meche-
len, where he spent much of his life as a devoted
mystic, composing a huge three-part manual,
the *Theologica Mystica*, as a guide for spiritual
progress toward the perfect life based on renun-
ciation and self-abasement. One of the greatest
Netherlandish Franciscans was Johannes Brugman of Nijmegen, another contemporary of Van
Eyck, who was renowned for his fervent preaching to the common folk in the open air.[6] It is
unlikely, however, that Jan van Eyck was directly
influenced by these mystics. His encounter with
the Franciscans and the story of the stigmata of
Saint Francis very likely came by way of his Italian patrons, the Adornes family in particular.[7] As
we shall see, Van Eyck's portrayal of the stigmatization of Saint Francis was an original conception and not derived from the traditional
iconography established by Tuscan artists in the
fourteenth century. But first it is important to

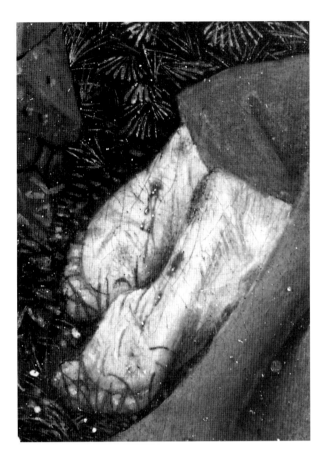

Fig. 97. Detail of the feet of Saint Francis from the Philadelphia *Saint Francis*.

review the *imitatio Christi* of Saint Francis as it is described in textual sources.[8]

The entire being of Francis was so dedicated to the imitation of Christ's humble and charitable way of life that his early biographers elaborated his *vita* into one that paralleled the ministry and Passion of Christ as related in the Gospels. Like Christ, Francis at first called twelve disciples to follow him. One later betrayed him, and another, a "doubting Thomas," believed in the stigmatization only after touching the wound in the chest of Francis. Many of the miracles and temptations of Francis recall those of Jesus, especially his identification with the Christ of the Passion, from the experiences in the Garden of Gethsemane to the Crucifixion, which was manifest from the earliest days of his conversion. In his life of the saint, Thomas of Celano tells us that after abandoning his rich parents and elegant home, Francis, "being now perfectly changed in heart (and soon to be changed in body too) . . . was walking one day by the church of S. Damian [near Assisi], which was almost ruinous, and was forsaken of all men. Led by the Spirit, he went in to pray. He fell down before the crucifix in devout supplication . . . and found himself a different man than he who had gone in. And, while he was thus moved, straightway—a thing unheard of for ages—the painted image of the Christ crucified

moved its lips and addressed him, calling him by name: 'Francis,' it said, 'Go repair My house, which as thou seest is wholly falling into ruin.'. . . He felt that the change he had undergone was ineffable, [and] it becomes us to be silent concerning that which he himself could not express. Thenceforth compassion for the Crucified was fixed in his holy soul, and (as we may piously suppose) the stigmata of the venerable Passion were deeply imprinted on his heart though not as yet on his flesh."[9]

Thomas of Celano also provides us with the earliest description of the miraculous experience of the stigmatization in 1224: "While he dwelt in the hermitage which . . . is called Alverna, two years before he gave back his soul to Heaven, he saw in a vision of God a man like a seraph having six wings, standing over him with hands outstretched and feet joined together, fixed to a cross. Two wings were raised above his head, two were spread out for flight, and two veiled the whole body. . . . He anxiously pondered what this vision might portend, and his spirit laboured sore to come to an understanding of it. And while he continued without any clear perception of its meaning, and the strangeness of the vision was perplexing his heart, marks of nails began to appear in his hands and feet, such as those he had seen a little while before in the Man crucified who had stood over him."[10]

In the slightly later Franciscan *Legenda Maior* of Saint Bonaventure, the importance of the *imitatio Christi* of Saint Francis is stressed by describing him as being "transformed" by his vision "into the likeness of Him Who of His exceeding love endured to be crucified." This happened, Bonaventure tells us, "on a certain morning about the Feast of the Exaltation of Holy Cross, while he was praying on the side of the mountain. . . . Accordingly, as the vision disappeared, it left in his heart a wondrous glow, but on his flesh also it imprinted a no less wondrous likeness of its tokens. For forthwith there began to appear in his hands and feet the marks of the nails, even as he had just beheld them in that Figure of the Crucified. . . . The right side, moreover, was—as if it had been pierced by a lance—seamed with a ruddy scar."[11]

The account of his life in the *Little Flowers* further elaborates the episode into "five considerations" of the meaning of the stigmatization. The first examines the significance of the holy mount of La Verna, property given to Francis by the nobleman Roland of Chiusi di Casentino, as a place, "most proper for devout contemplation . . . very solitary and meet for those that desire to do penance in a place far away from the world." The next considers how Francis, with three friars (including Brother Leo), then set out for La Verna and how Francis marveled at the form of the towering mountain with its "great clefts and caverns in the mighty rocks," which are likened to the rocks rent asunder at the very hour of Christ's death on the cross (Matthew 27:51). The stigmatization is described and interpreted in detail in the third consideration. In the fervor of his intense contemplation of the Passion, Francis "was wholly changed into Jesus." Then, after the vision of Christ spoke to Francis, "the marks of the nails began anon to be seen on the hands and on the feet of St. Francis, in the same manner as he had then seen them in the body of Jesus Christ crucified . . . in the form of a seraph."[12] The final considerations are interpretations of later miracles connected with the stigmata.

The complete transformation of Francis into Christ is further elaborated in the *Actus beati Francisci et sociorum eius*, from the early fourteenth century, describing Francis as the Second Christ (*Franciscus alter Christus*). This compelling concept—*Franciscus alter Christus*—was later expanded into typological parallels between the narratives of the lives of Christ and Francis in the controversial *Liber de conformitate vitae beati Francisci ad vitam Domini Jesu* written by Bartholomeus of Pisa between 1385 and 1390 and presented to the Chapter General at Assisi in 1399.[13]

The consummate representation of the stigmatization of Saint Francis in Italian painting was created by Giotto in the Bardi Chapel in Santa Croce, Florence (fig. 98).[14] Posed frontally, Francis rises on one leg from a kneeling position and turns sharply to the right, raising his arms above him as he peers up intently at the image of the Crucifix affixed to a six-winged seraph with rays of light descending from the wounds of Christ to his hands, feet, and side. The setting, La Verna, is reduced to a barren plateau backed by steep, unadorned cliffs. To the far right is the small cell in the form of a chapel erected for Francis; to the left can be seen a dark cleft in the mountain, perhaps a reference to the hollow in the rocks that miraculously appeared as a refuge

Fig. 98. Giotto (Italian, d. 1337), *The Stigmatization of Saint Francis*, fresco, Bardi Chapel, Santa Croce, Florence.

for Francis when tempted by the devil preceding the stigmatization.[15] Minor changes in the iconography appear in the Giottesque fresco in the Upper Church at Assisi (fig. 99). While facing the vision, Francis kneels in three-quarter view and assumes the same orant position with arms held out and upward to receive the stigmata. To the far right, across a deep crevice in the landscape, appears Brother Leo, reading and seated on the ground before a small basilica. In both frescoes, the figure of Francis with arms cast upward and to the sides was no doubt meant to repeat the form of Christ on the cross. The dramatic turning of the body, the head tossed back, and the direct confrontation with the seraphic vision whose rays of light transfer the stigmata to the saint's hands, feet, and side, established the traditional iconographic types (with or without Brother Leo) for later Italian versions.

Representations of the stigmatization of Saint Francis are very rare in Netherlandish art. Aside from Van Eyck's version, the only significant examples are found in the oeuvre of Gerard David (fig. 100) and in a few depictions of the stigmatization found in Books of Hours.[16] In these, the general pose of Saint Francis in ecstasy follows that of Giotto's painting, with

Fig. 99. Giotto and workshop, *The Stigmatization of Saint Francis*, fresco, Upper Church, Basilica of Saint Francis, Assisi.

Fig. 100. Gerard David (Netherlandish, d. 1523), *The Stigmatization of Saint Francis*, panel, 18 x 6½" (45.7 x 16.5 cm), The Metropolitan Museum of Art, New York, The Michael Friedsam Collection, bequest of Michael Friedsam, 1931, 32.100.40c.

hands outstretched and face lifted to the vision as the marks of the wounds descend along rays of light. Furthermore, in these few Northern examples, the setting is a rustic woodland, sometimes with a small chapel in the distance. Even in later Northern panels where Saint Francis appears amid other saints on altarpiece side wings, he assumes the same orant pose in either a kneeling or standing position.[17]

Van Eyck's *Saint Francis Receiving the Stigmata* differs markedly from those in the Giottesque tradition. It seems curious, at first, that the theatrical pose of Giotto's Francis should be rejected by Van Eyck. Instead, he portrayed Francis in profile kneeling silently in prayer and, as a number of scholars have pointed out, seeming to stare past the hovering apparition of the seraph-Christ (fig. 101). Curious, too, are the omissions (or concealment?) of the wound in the side of Francis and the rays of light descending from the crucified Christ to mark the wounds, essential features of the iconography. Infrared reflectographs of the Turin panel, in fact, indicate that originally Van Eyck's Francis wore sandals or some form of footwear (faint underdrawings of such have been detected on the feet), which would have concealed the wounds there as well.[18]

Even more striking is the dramatic landscape setting for the stigmatization with its colorful outcroppings of rocks that frame a panoramic view of a deep river valley and a distant city. Traditionally, La Verna, the retreat for the saint's meditation, had been indicated sparingly. Steep, barren hills form the setting for Giotto's fresco

in Santa Croce; the jagged rises in the Assisi fresco are clearly derived from the archaic Italo-Byzantine cracked-rock or basalt formations common in Byzantine desert landscapes. In fifteenth-century representations in the North, the settings for hermit saints—Saints John the Baptist, Anthony, Jerome, and so forth—are usually rendered as cozy woodland clearings with few, if any, specific marks of identification. Such are the landscape backgrounds of David's versions of the stigmatization of Saint Francis. Van Eyck, on the other hand, offers us a unique landscape appropriate for the Franciscan legend. Francis and Brother Leo are placed on a shallow plateau placed high in a mountainous landscape and framed by unusual rock formations. To the left, directly behind Francis, appear grayish green igneous rocks, weathered and cracked, much as those found behind the processions of hermit and pilgrim saints in the side panels of the Ghent altarpiece. To the right, however, a new rock formation appears (fig. 102). The eye-catching cliff with its pronounced horizontal striations and layers of sedimentary sandstone, etched and corroded, with various fossil and carbonate concretions, is no doubt meant to represent a specific site, the rugged La Verna, the wilderness retreat of Francis high and apart from the rest of the world, the perfect refuge for the hermit saint.[19] A sparkling brook gushes from the lower bed of sandstone, its waters washing across smaller limestone boulders and pebbles. The setting brings to mind the beautiful landscape in Giovanni Bellini's famous *Stigmatization of Saint Francis* in the Frick Collection, New York, with its towering cliff and broad valley with a small village in the far distance (fig. 103). One can, in fact, characterize Van Eyck's setting as one of the earliest examples of a "hermit" or "anchorite" landscape in Northern art, establishing a convention that would culminate in the eerie backdrops of sixteenth-century paintings of hermit saints, such as those by Gossaert, Patinir, Grünewald, and Altdorfer, where the barren desert setting is further emphasized as a sterile and rugged tract of land that will soon blossom into a verdant garden.[20]

Where would Van Eyck get the idea for these horizontally layered hills of sandstone? Earlier generations of scholars, who believed that the Philadelphia painting was executed early, speculated that the idea struck Jan during his sojourn in Spain and Portugal, 1428–29, and that he was inspired by the dramatic Pyrenees or, more specifically, Mont Serrat.[21] W. H. James Weale identified one of the prominent plants in the foreground as the palmetto, a species of flora he could have seen in Iberia, and he stated that the tan-gray habit of Francis was an anomaly, as it befitted the Reformed Franciscans in Spain and not the Gray Friars of the

Netherlands.[22] Finally, the fact that the painting was purchased in Lisbon about 1830 is further cited as evidence for the Spanish origin of the work. These arguments are not convincing for a number of reasons, especially since we know that Jan often employed motifs earlier observed in Spain in paintings executed long after his return from Iberia in 1429.

Fig. 101. Detail of the Philadelphia *Saint Francis*.

Fig. 102. Detail of the Philadelphia *Saint Francis*.

Fig. 103. Giovanni Bellini (Italian, d. 1516), *The Stigmatization of Saint Francis*, late 1470s, panel, 48¹³⁄₁₆ x 55⅞" (124 x 142 cm), The Frick Collection, New York.

placed in a subordinate position (see fig. 100). In Van Eyck's painting Leo not only figures prominently—he occupies the entire right side of the composition—but he shares equally the same frontal plane with Francis. We shall return to this problem shortly.

It should seem clear by now that Van Eyck's painting of the stigmatization differs considerably from the traditional representations, so much so that one wonders what sources he drew upon. One could, of course, review all the pertinent textual sources, those of Thomas of Celano, Bonaventure, the anonymous author of the *Little Flowers*, even the account of Jacopo Voragine in the *Legenda Aurea*, but to my knowledge none of these provides the clues for Van Eyck's departures from the tradition. Perhaps Van Eyck's patron (possibly the elder Adornes?) informed the painter of the rudimentary lines of the story, emphasizing the seraphic vision, the desert setting, and the companionship of Brother Leo, but this idea is mere hypothesis. However, one can offer some plausible arguments for the more personal and allusive nature of Van Eyck's interpretation, particularly regarding the response of Francis to the vision and the curious omission of certain details. To be sure, Jan van Eyck does not seem to be an artist attuned to the world of the ascetic mystic hermit, who held poverty and humility as primary virtues of behavior. Van Eyck lived in the very precious and richly adorned world of the Burgundian court, as the honored painter (*varlet de chambre*) of Philip the Good. His life, furthermore, revolved about the intellectual core of the court, and he was, as Philip the Good himself informed us, acclaimed for his knowledge of science and letters.

Art historians have frequently found intrinsic analogies between the artist's imagery and the religious philosophies of his time. Thus, Van Eyck's art has sometimes been characterized as an expression in paint of the thinking of the Nominalists because his incredible eye focused so sharply on physical realities. Van Eyck's "microscopic-telescopic" vision, as Panofsky so aptly characterized it, can be meaningfully compared to the Nominalists' quest for the basic truths residing in the particulars. But he has also been likened to the Scholastics insofar as his very real world veils multileveled meanings in the form of "disguised symbols," to borrow another idea from Panofsky. The Madonna can

But do these rock protrusions above Leo resemble the Pyrenees? I think not. They do, however, bear a striking resemblance to the striated cliffs of La Verna, and it has been argued that Jan van Eyck must have known the hallowed site firsthand or through some reliable source.[23] How appropriate and consistent with Jan's realism! Furthermore, whatever the site and the source, we know that Van Eyck's new addition to the vocabulary of dramatic landscape had an immediate impact in both the North and in Italy. It has been pointed out that the rocky cliff behind the shed in the *Adoration of the Magi*, c. 1475, by Botticelli, in the London National Gallery (fig. 104), is an exact copy of the curious landscape behind Brother Leo; and other, less specific, references to Van Eyck's dramatic rocky cliffs of layered stone can be found in the sketches of Leonardo da Vinci.[24]

Curious, too, is the prominence of Brother Leo who sits huddled on the ground with his back to Francis, asleep and unaware of the seraphic vision. His presence as a companion of Francis is discussed at some length in the texts, especially in the *Little Flowers*, and he sometimes appears in Giottesque versions (fig. 98) sitting apart and reading the Gospels during which time Francis, isolated from him in the landscape, experiences the stigmatization. In the few Northern versions, Leo usually sleeps, but is

Fig. 104. Detail of *The Adoration of the Magi*, c. 1470–75, by Sandro Botticelli (Italian, 1445–1510), panel, 19¹¹/₁₆ x 53½" (50 x 136 cm), National Gallery, London, no. 592.

represent the Church, or vice versa, the church can be an attribute of the Madonna; a seemingly accurate topographical landscape can be the Heavenly Jerusalem on another level of meaning; transitions in the styles of architectural elevations can represent the confluence of the Old and New Testaments in doctrine; details such as carved capitals can be viewed as decoration or as subtle pictorial footnotes for some higher and more intricate content in his paintings. These components of Van Eyck's art hardly bespeak the Franciscan temperament, but I would like to add to these analogies another that is rarely noted: the passivity of the mystical experiences of his people when portrayed in devotional attitudes. In many ways, Jan van Eyck was a genius of his time, a consummate artist who rose far above the theologians, philosophers, and the literati of his day in that he so vividly placed before our eyes the whole model of Christian thought, belief, and experience in a single picture. Let me cite a few examples.

Much has been written about the complex iconography of the *Virgin of Chancellor Rolin* in the Louvre (fig. 105). The highly detailed river landscape has invited several interpretations as to whether it is an actual site—Bruges, Liège,

Maastricht, Geneva, and so forth—or a symbolic cityscape. One major point of controversy focuses on the foreground setting. The marbled pavilion usually has been identified as the throne room of the Virgin on high, and one wonders how the chancellor could so boldly enter Mary's tribune and confront her without the benefit of a patron saint to introduce him, as was customary. This is unprecedented. But is Rolin visiting the Virgin or is she visiting Rolin in his chamber in the form of a vision? Her throne is set at an angle—unusual for a throne room—and, furthermore, Rolin, clearly reciting his devotions at the *prie-dieu*, stares right past the Madonna and Child! Mary is not placed in the line of his vision, but behind it. Van Eyck thus presents us with Rolin's mystical vision of the Madonna and Child as the manifestation of his devotion in very concrete, Nominalistic terms. He further elaborates the world of the donor and that of the Virgin in the eye-catching details of the backgrounds behind them, emphatically splitting the symbolic world in two, the more mundane behind the earthly patron, the more ecclesiastical behind the Virgin and Child.[25]

The Madonna and Child likewise appear as a vision behind the kneeling Canon van der

Paele in the famous painting in Bruges, where, on either side of the vision, the two worlds of Paele's domain, that of the priestly and that of the militant church, are personified in the figures of the priest Saint Donatus (the patron of his church) and the warrior Saint George (his name saint), and then are elaborated throughout in the carvings of the capitals. The Virgin and Child, the mystical presence of his devotion, thus appear as the total Church that subsumes these worlds.

Let us now return to our Saint Francis. He, too, kneels in meditation in his retreat in La Verna. His praying hands appear on the central axis of the picture, splitting the composition into two antithetical halves. To the right is the slumbering Brother Leo, an image of sloth in monastic life, turned aside from the seraphic vision and closed off by the barren rocks from which only a bubbling spring promises salvation and rejuvenation. To the left, Saint Francis kneels before a cluster of plants and ferns with green trees and bushes and a radiant river valley in the distance. It no longer seems so unusual that Francis does not even focus on the appari-

tion or that he is unmoved by it. This is Van Eyck's world. As in the portrayals of the Chancellor Rolin or the Canon van der Paele, Francis stares hypnotically right past his vision, which hovers at a slight distance behind him. He is not struck down by the impact of the stigmatization; rather, he is being silently informed by it. How else would Van Eyck have expressed such a subtle mystical experience? Not even in the panoramic *Adoration of the Lamb* in the Ghent altarpiece do his people respond theatrically to the apocalyptic visions (fig. 106). In this respect, the static and frozen appearance of Saint Francis is wholly in keeping with Van Eyck's expression. And is not this interpretation more in keeping with the spirit of the stigmatization of Saint Francis where, it will be recalled, Thomas of Celano and others inform us that after having the vision of the Man as seraph, Francis "pondered what this vision might portend . . . . And while he continued without any clear perception of its meaning . . . marks of nails *began* to appear in his hands and feet, such as those *he had seen a little while before* in the Man crucified who had stood over him."[26]

This raises a very important point concerning the ingenuity of Jan van Eyck. Could it be that Jan's original representation was that of the mystical vision experienced by Saint Francis *before* the stigmatization actually occurred? A more accurate title for the painting would thus have been "Saint Francis and His Vision of the Crucified Christ." Informed of the traditional significance of the miraculous stigmatization on La Verna (by his patron?), Jan then altered his painting by removing the sandals and adding the marks of the nails to the hands and feet. If so, this interpretation of Van Eyck's working procedure would serve as a happy concurrence between the findings of the art historian and those of the specialist in laboratory analysis of his paintings. J.R.J. van Asperen de Boer writes: "That the feet of Saint Francis were first underdrawn with some form of footwear and did not show the stigmata was an iconographical error, which the artist corrected during painting. Such corrections have been shown to have occurred in the genesis of the Ghent altarpiece as well and could be taken as typically Eyckian."[27] Was this originally, however, an "iconographical error" or a conception of a more precise moment in the experiences of the saint on La Verna as Jan understood the story?

There remains another vexing question, unavoidable for art historians, as to what pictorial model or models Van Eyck may have turned to for this unusual image of the hermit saint and his mystical vision in the wilderness. It seems unlikely that Van Eyck was aware of the Giottesque traditions for the stigmatization of Saint Francis. I feel that Van Eyck could have produced this work based only on the rudiments of the Franciscan legend, perhaps delivered to him orally, but there were other familiar compositions that could have inspired him. One could argue that representations of the Vision of the Burning Bush experienced by Moses, the saint's Old Testament counterpart, provided a fitting model (compare the painting by Dierick Bouts in the Johnson Collection; fig. 107), but while such typology is commonplace in Franciscan literature,[28] it would seem more appropriate to look for a similar parallel within the life of Christ, since, as we have seen, *Franciscus alter Christus* (Francis the Second Christ) was another, even more compelling image in the texts.

What episode then? Certainly no Crucifixion

provides us with the elements of this simple composition, and the Transfiguration—another type for the stigmatization of Saint Francis—is also composed along very different lines. The one episode that Van Eyck knew well in the Passion of Christ that could have served as a prototype for Francis's mystical vision is the Prayer of Christ in the Garden of Gethsemane, where not only would a good precedent for the sleeping Leo be found, but also where the mystery of the vision, the Eucharistic chalice, has the appropriate overtones for the image of the crucified Christ experienced by Francis. A somewhat similar composition for the Prayer in the Garden of Gethsemane can be found, in fact, in the Eyckian miniatures (Master H) of the Turin-Milan Hours (fig. 108).[29] Perhaps it is not even necessary to seek out such prototypes. Van Eyck's genius alone could explain the mystery of his *Saint Francis Receiving the Stigmata.*

Fig. 107. Attributed to Dierick Bouts (Netherlandish, d. 1475), *Moses and the Burning Bush, with Moses Removing His Shoes,* c. 1465–70, panel, 17⅝ x 14" (44.8 x 35.6 cm), Philadelphia Museum of Art, John G. Johnson Collection, cat. 339.

Fig. 108. *Christ in the
Garden of Gethsemane*,
illuminated page from the
Turin-Milan Hours,
c. 1440–45, 11 x 7½"
(28 x 19 cm), Museo
Civico d'Arte Antica,
Turin, fol. 30v.

Detail of fig. 108.

1. For a brief summary of these issues see "The Philadelphia and Turin Paintings: The Literature and Controversy over Attribution" by Joseph J. Rishel in this volume.

2. Erwin Panofsky, *Early Netherlandish Painting: Its Origins and Character* (Cambridge, Mass., 1953), vol. 1, p. 192, n. 1. As early as 1906, Karl Voll, *Die altniederländische Malerei von Jan van Eyck bis Memling* (Leipzig, 1906), vol. 1, p. 48, expressed a similar sentiment, stating that the legend of the stigmatization is so misunderstood Jan cannot be considered the author.

3. Charles D. Cuttler, *Northern Painting from Pucelle to Bruegel: Fourteenth, Fifteenth, and Sixteenth Centuries* (New York, 1968), p. 103.

4. Giorgio T. Faggin, *The Complete Paintings of the Van Eycks* (New York, 1968), p. 89, no. 5.

5. John R. H. Moorman, *A History of the Franciscan Order from Its Origins until the Year 1517* (Oxford, 1968), pp. 443, 542–44.

6. See P. F. Servais Dirks, *Histoire littéraire et bibliographique des Frères Mineurs de l'observance de St.-François en Belgique et dans les Pays-Bays* (Antwerp, 1885); Benjamin de Troeyer, *Bio-Bibliographia Franciscana Neerlandica ante saeculum XVI*, 3 vols. (Nieuwkoop, 1974). For further bibliography of Franciscans in Bruges, see A. Vanhoutryve, *Bibliografie van de Geschiedenis van Brugge* (Bruges, 1972), pp. 159, 162, 457–59. For Hendrik Herp, see L. Verschueren, *Hendrik Herp: Spiegel der Volcomenheit* (Antwerp, 1931); and A. de Sérent, "Histoire littéraire de trois mystiques Franciscans," *Études Françaises*, vol. 44 (1932), pp. 717ff. For Johannes Brugman, see W. Moll, *Johannes Brugman en het godsdienstig leven onzer vaderen in de vijftiende eeuw*, 2 vols. (Amsterdam, 1854).

7. The troublesome connections of the two paintings with the family of Anselme Adornes are reviewed by Joseph J. Rishel in "The Philadelphia and Turin Paintings: The Literaure and Controversy over Attribution," in this volume. It has sometimes been argued that Saint Francis is a portrait of the patron (Anselme Adornes, however, was only seventeen years old at Van Eyck's death); see Valentin Denis, *Tutta la pittura di Jan van Eyck* (Milan, 1954), p. 36.

8. The basic sources are *Vita Prima S. Francisci* (c. 1228–29) and *Vita Secunda S. Francisci* (c. 1244–47) by Thomas of Celano [see Thomas of Celano, *The Lives of S. Francis of Assisi*, trans. A. G. Ferrers Howell (London, 1908)]; *Legenda Maior* (1260–63) by Saint Bonaventure [see *The Life of Saint Francis by Saint Bonaventura*, trans. E. Gurney Salter (London, 1904); this translation is reprinted in *The Little Flowers of St. Francis; The Mirror of Perfection; The Life of St. Francis by St. Bonaventure* (New York and London, 1951), with the section *The Little Flowers of St. Francis*, trans. T. Okey]; *Actus beati Francisci et sociorum eius* (early 14th century); and *Liber de conformitate vitae beati Francisci ad vitam Domini Jesu* by Bartholomeus of Pisa (c. 1390). For a compilation of these and other sources, see Marion A. Habig, ed., *St. Francis of Assisi: Writings and Early Biographies: English Omnibus of the Sources for the Life of St. Francis*, 4th rev. ed. (Chicago, 1983). Also see John R. H. Moorman, *The Sources for the Life of Saint Francis of Assisi* (Manchester, 1940).

9. Thomas of Celano, *The Second Life*, in Howell, trans., 1908, pp. 153–54 (see note 8 above).

10. Thomas of Celano, *The First Life*, in Howell, trans., 1908, pp. 92–93.

11. Saint Bonaventure, *The Life of St. Francis*, in Salter, trans., 1951, pp. 507–8.

12. *The Little Flowers of St. Francis*, in Okey, trans., 1951, pp. 129, 136, 147, 149.

13. See the excellent article by H. W. van Os, "Saint Francis of Assisi as a Second Christ in Early Italian Painting," *Simiolus*, vol. 7, no. 3 (1974), pp. 115–32. Compare E. James Mundy, "*Franciscus alter Christus*: The Intercessory Function of a Late Quattrocento Panel," *Record of the Art Museum, Princeton University*, vol. 36, no. 2 (1977), pp. 4–15. For a basic study of these texts, see Stanislas da Campagnola, *L'angelo del sesto sigillo e l'alter Christus* (Rome, 1971), esp. pp. 202–5.

14. For this and other trecento examples, see John R. H. Moorman, *Early Franciscan Art and Literature* (Manchester, 1943); George Kaftal, *Saint Francis in Italian Painting* (London, 1950); Leonetto Tintori and Millard Meiss, *The Paintings of the Life of Saint Francis in Assisi* (New York, 1962). For pre-Giotto paintings in Tuscany, see Kaftal, *The Iconography of the Saints in Tuscan Painting* (Florence, 1952), pp. 395ff. An excellent survey of the iconography of Saint Francis in general is the entry "Franz (Franziskus) von Assisi" by O. Schmucki and Gerlach van 's-Hertogenbosch in *Lexikon der christlichen Ikonographie*, ed. Wolfgang Braunfels (Rome, 1974), vol. 6, cols. 260–315; and Alfonso Pompei and Lorenzo Di Fonzo, "Francesco da Assisi," in *Bibliotheca sanctorum* (Rome, 1964), vol. 5, cols. 1052–1150.

15. See *The Little Flowers of St. Francis*, in Okey, trans., 1951, p. 141.

16. For example, *The Stigmatization of Saint Francis*, by the Boucicaut Master, Musée Jacquemart-André, Paris, MS 2, fol. 37v.

17. See Max J. Friedländer, *The Van Eycks—Petrus Christus*, vol. 1 of *Early Netherlandish Painting*, trans. Heinz Norden (Leiden and Brussels, 1967): Francis appears standing beside the Madonna enthroned in the Frankfurt altar by Petrus Christus (vol. 1, pl. 78); he appears standing in the left wing of the Sforza altar in Brussels by a follower of Rogier van der Weyden (vol. 2, pl. 109); and in several works by Gerard David and his followers (vol. 6, part 2, pls. 174, 185, 254, 258, 269, 292). Most early woodcuts with Francis are German in origin; see R. S. Field, *Fifteenth-Century Woodcuts and Metalcuts from the National Gallery of Art, Washington, D.C.* (Washington, D.C., 1965), nos. 224–27. For the illumination in the Boucicaut Hours and related miniatures, see Millard Meiss, *French Painting in the Time of Jean de Berry: The Boucicaut Master* (London, 1968), pp. 131–33. For a list of these representations, see *Lexikon der christlichen Ikonographie*, vol. 6, col. 298 (see note 14 above).

18. See "Some Technical Observations on the Turin and Philadelphia Versions of 'Saint Francis Receiving the Stigmata'" by J.R.J. van Asperen de Boer in this volume.

19. See, however, "Geological Aspects of Jan van Eyck's 'Saint Francis Receiving the Stigmata'" by Kenneth Bé in this volume.

20. For Bellini's painting, see Millard Meiss, *Giovanni Bellini's Saint Francis in the Frick Collection* (New York,

1964); and J. V. Fleming, *From Bonaventure to Bellini—An Essay in Franciscan Exegeses* (Princeton, 1982), esp. pp. 32–74. For discussion of the "hermit" or "anchorite" landscape, see Pierre Bonnard, "La Signification du désert, selon le Nouveau Testament," *Hommage et reconnaissance: Recueil de travaux publiés à l'occasion du soixantième anniversaire de Karl Barth* (Neuchâtel, 1946), pp. 9–18.

21. W. H. James Weale first published his ideas on the Spanish origin of the Philadelphia painting in the London *Times*, February 3, 1886, p. 7. See also Weale's *Hubert and John van Eyck: Their Life and Work* (London and New York, 1908), pp. 130–35. For further arguments along this line, see August L. Mayer, "A Jan van Eyck Problem," *The Burlington Magazine*, vol. 48 (1926), p. 200; August F. Jaccaci, "Mr. Johnson's Van Eyck," *The Burlington Magazine*, vol. 11 (1907), pp. 46–48; and Chandler Post, *History of Spanish Painting* (Cambridge, Mass., 1900), vol. 4, pt. 1, pp. 20–21.

22. R. Huber (*A Documented History of the Franciscan Order* [Washington, D.C., 1944], pp. 683ff.), states that gray was the declared color of the Franciscan habit, but that different colors were often used because the garments were acquired through alms and other outside contributions. He further states that there is no evidence of brown being the official color until the late seventeenth century (p. 687). The habit worn by Francis in the Philadelphia painting is not completely brown but also gray brown or light tan. Even if Weale is right about the Spanish Franciscans, that would not be convincing evidence of the painting's Spanish origin. Jan van Eyck frequently incorporated Spanish elements into his paintings after his trip there in 1428–29; see James Snyder, "Jan van Eyck and Adam's Apple," *The Art Bulletin*, vol. 58 (1976), pp. 511–15.

23. Already in 1888, Henri Hymans ("Le Saint François d'Assise de Jean van Eyck," *Gazette des Beaux-Arts*, 2nd period, vol. 37 [1888], p. 82) declared the city in the background to be "parfaitement reconnissable" as Assisi.

Charles Sterling ("Jan van Eyck avant 1432," *Revue de l'Art*, no. 33 [1976], p. 29) stated that the setting is "Sasso delle Sitmmate [*sic*] à la Verna."

24. Günter Panhans, "Florentiner Maler verarbeiten ein eyckisches Bild," *Wiener Jahrbuch für Kunstgeschichte*, vol. 27 (1974), pp. 188–98. For the influence on Leonardo, see also E. H. Gombrich, *The Heritage of Apelles: Studies in the Art of the Renaissance* (Ithaca, 1976), pp. 33–34.

25. For the diverse theories concerning the iconography of the Rolin Madonna, see Panofsky, 1953, vol. 1, pp. 192ff.; James Snyder, "Jan van Eyck and the Madonna of Chancellor Nicolas Rolin," *Oud Holland*, vol. 82 (1967), pp. 163–71; H. Roosen-Runge, *Die Rolin-Madonna des Jan van Eyck* (Wiesbaden, 1972); Anne Hagopian van Buren, "The Canonical Office in Renaissance Painting II: More About the Rolin *Madonna*," *The Art Bulletin*, vol. 60 (1978), pp. 617–33; and Carol J. Purtle, *The Marian Paintings of Jan van Eyck* (Princeton, 1982), pp. 59ff.

26. Thomas of Cclano, *The First Life*, in Howell, trans., 1908, p. 93. Italics are the author's.

27. "Some Technical Observations on the Turin and Philadelphia Versions of 'Saint Francis Receiving the Stigmata" by J.R.J. van Asperen de Boer in this volume.

28. Compare Fleming, 1982, esp. pp. 32ff., for these and other parallels.

29. Albert Châtelet, *Early Dutch Painting: Painting in the Northern Netherlands in the Fifteenth Century*, trans. Christopher Brown and Anthony Turner (Amsterdam, 1981), pp. 39–44, pp. 200–201 [no. 30] attributes the Philadelphia painting to the Master of Hand H: "The painting exhibits close parallels with the *Jesus in the Garden of Gethsemane* from *Milan-Turin* [see fig. 108]: the same structure of the landscape, the same manner of placing the figures, and the similarity of the silhouettes, whether of Christ and St. Francis or of the sleeping apostles and the Franciscan friar."

Kenneth Bé

Geological Aspects of Jan van Eyck's "Saint Francis Receiving the Stigmata"

The detailed rock formations in the Philadelphia *Saint Francis Receiving the Stigmata* (pl. I), attributed to Jan van Eyck, distinguish this work as an exceptionally fine example of natural realism in fifteenth-century Netherlandish art.[1] Yet, in the vast literature on this painting, there is a paucity of scientifically correct observation; indeed, few writers have remarked in particular on the prominence of the rock formations in the landscape.[2] In addition to the superb detail of the rocks themselves, a wide lithological variety has been brought together and juxtaposed within this tiny composition. For the present-day geologist, the details, colors, textures, and morphologies in Van Eyck's rendering of rocks yield a plethora of scientifically accurate information.[3] Identifying the individual rock types and assessing the entire outcrops and their spatial relationship may provide some insight into Van Eyck's method for deriving this landscape composition. In a broader perspective, one might also speculate on how rock details and large-scale formations convey significant meaning in paintings.

Geological Aspects

Four distinct rock types are depicted in this painting: in the right foreground are several detached limestone boulders; behind them, a stratified sedimentary sequence; in the left middle ground, an igneous outcrop; and in the distance, a pair of jagged peaks. The last are fanciful forms similar in appearance to small rock specimens propped in upright positions (fig. 109). Painted in a manner typical of landscape views of the fifteenth and sixteenth centuries, such renderings recall Cennino Cennini's advice to artists to copy rock samples brought into the studio when modeling mountains in paintings.[4]

The boulders in the foreground (fig. 110) are identifiable as limestone from their rounded shapes and the abundance of clearly discernible shell fossils contained within. Although fossils are present in a wide variety of sedimentary rocks, limestone more often contains such intact fossil shells. The rounded appearance of limestone results from the weathering dissolution of carbonate material. Because of its internal texture, weathered sandstone can be similar in shape, but would be far less likely to contain unbroken fossils. The boulders in this painting are dark reddish brown, an indication of iron content or dark mineral impurities.

Fig. 111. Detail of the boulders to the right of Brother Leo in the Philadelphia *Saint Francis*.

Fig. 109. Detail of the rocky peaks in the Philadelphia *Saint Francis*.

Fig. 110. Detail of the boulders in the foreground of the Philadelphia *Saint Francis*.

Several features can be noted about the fossils. The boulder at the lower left of figure 111 contains crescent-shaped forms, the result of the rock face intersecting the fossils to reveal cross sections of the shells in side profile. The other large boulder displays closed loops, resulting from intersections along the face of the shell halves—perpendicular, in other words, to the other boulder. The pattern of the fossil shells in this boulder also indicates that the rock was overturned from its original depositional orientation. Shell halves are generally moved by water currents so that their convex sides face upward. The majority of the fossil shells in this boulder are painted concave side up, confirming its upside-down orientation.

Precise identification of the shelled organisms in the painting is impossible. Most likely, they are a type of mollusk similar to present-day clams (pelecypods). Alternatively, they could belong to another group of shelled fauna called brachiopods, also commonly encountered in the fossil record. It should be noted, however, that fossils found in limestone are invariably of marine origin.

Horizontal layering of rocks (stratification) is a feature typical of sedimentary rocks that results from the flat deposition of sediment over older sediment beds. Van Eyck has painted two kinds of interlayered sedimentary lithologies, sandstone and shale, with remarkable clarity.[5] Directly behind the pile of limestone boulders is a unit of shale (fig. 111). Although partially obscured by Brother Leo's shadow, this layer is distinguished by closely spaced parallel, horizontal joints. Shale is a fine-grained rock formed by the deposition of a high proportion of platelike minerals (such as mica) in quiet waters. The horizontal deposition of such minerals causes shales to develop such tightly spaced joints (fissility). Van Eyck has also accurately depicted the tendency for more coherent zones of shale to remain intact while surrounding weaker zones are pervasively jointed. The orange tint in one of the shale layers indicates a rich iron content within that zone.

The large slab immediately above the shale is a massive layer of sandstone (fig. 112). Sandstone is predominantly composed of round, weathered grains of quartz. In the painting the sandstone is accurately rendered with a uniformly weathered, rounded surface, punctuated by several faintly defined horizontal breaks. In contrast to the shale, this unit is lighter in color. Sandstone is more resistant to weathering than shale, which explains why the sandstone layer forms the prominent ledge protruding over the shale. Within the sandstone, Van Eyck has painted subtle color changes in several horizontal bands. Most prominent is the light orange band, again indicative of a higher iron content, in the center of the sandstone. Accompanying the color change are numerous small, irregularly shaped cavities scattered throughout this zone. These appear to be the sites of weathered-out inclusions, either fossil fragments or carbonate nodules. They closely resemble the fossil cavities in the sample in figure 113.

Overlying the sandstone unit are several thinner, interlayered beds of shale and sandstone similar in appearance to those already discussed. This section is partially obscured from view by loose boulders of sandstone (fig. 112). The sideways position of these sandstones is curious, suggesting that they were placed there on purpose. One interesting surface detail is the X-shaped pattern of scratch marks on one of the boulders.[6] While one cannot rule out the possibility that these may be depictions of graffiti or quarrying tool marks, perhaps they were included by the artist to render the tactile surface qualities of the sandstone.

Overall, the stratified sequence described is geologically revealing. The abrupt changes between shale and sandstone and the modest thickness of the sandstone layer indicate that Van Eyck has depicted a flysch or turbidite sequence.[7] This is a kind of sedimentary layering sequence deposited in the margins of marine basins, where intervals of steady, quiescent

Fig. 112. Detail of the rock formation behind Brother Leo in the Philadelphia *Saint Francis.*

deposition of shale sediment are punctuated by onslaughts of rapid sand deposition by underwater mud slides (turbidity currents).[8] The relative thicknesses of the two lithologies vary randomly in precisely the way shown in the painting.

The perfect horizontality of the rock strata in the painting indicates that they were never disturbed by later crustal movements. Although it is impossible to determine a specific location for the strata depicted in the painting, a mountainous region such as the Alps is improbable, even though an Alpine vista is present in the distance. In such a region, rock strata have generally been tilted, overturned, and folded. It is possible that the strata belong to the area that geologists call the Paris Basin, which covers most of France and southern Flanders. It should be emphasized that the outcrop is surely not representative of the Sasso di Stimmate at La Verna, the traditional site of Saint Francis's stigmatization (fig. 114).[9]

The next rock outcrop in the painting, to the left of Saint Francis (fig. 115), sharply contrasts to those previously discussed, both visually and

Fig. 113. Fossil cavities in limestone.

Fig. 114. View of Sasso di Stimmate, La Verna.

Fig. 115. Detail of the rocks behind Saint Francis in the Philadelphia *Saint Francis*.

lithologically. This is identifiable as an igneous rock on the basis of its hard, massive form and irregular joint pattern. The dark gray color indicates a basalt, a dark, intrusive rock of magmatic origin. The faint orange color applied by the artist in several places is typical of the weathered patina of oxidized iron on such rocks. The irregular pattern of joints results from weathering along zones of weakness predetermined by the

cooling history of the rock. Such intrusions may also develop at least one predominant orientation of parallel joints as can be seen on the left half of the outcrop in Van Eyck's work.

The small outcrop at the left edge of the painting behind the feet of Saint Francis (fig. 116) is more difficult to identify, since it shares features with both the limestone boulders and the basaltic outcrop, although it is closer in appearance to the latter. The circular patterns on its upper surface might be Van Eyck's rendering of lichen growths.

The juxtaposition of an isolated basaltic outcrop adjacent to an undisturbed sedimentary sequence is geologically unlikely. It is therefore evident that Van Eyck's landscape elements derive from separate studies of outcrops encountered individually.[10] The artist then assembled them into a single landscape in close proximity, although constituting a disparate ensemble.

Van Eyck's achievement in rendering rocks as they appear in nature is remarkable when one considers the state of geology as a science from the Middle Ages. Van Eyck's detailed, empirical understanding of the visual aspects of rocks should be considered in the context of the prevailing theories speculating on the origin of stones. Certainly, the prominent rock formations in paintings by Van Eyck and his contemporaries

must have evoked in the viewer the enigmas of divine creation in nature, since by the fifteenth century in Europe it was widely believed that rocks formed under divine celestial influences.[11]

Paleontology in the Early Fifteenth Century
The earliest writings on close field observation of fossils in Western Europe date from several generations after the time of Van Eyck.[12] The ancient Greeks had correctly proposed, however, that petrified shells found inland were originally deposited during past inundations from the sea, but by the eleventh century it was widely believed that fossils were formed *in situ* within the rocks in which they were found. It was also speculated that fossils were the remains of "failed" attempts in the production of life; in other words, they were abandoned works of God, a theologically satisfying conclusion.

Another explanation held that fossils were the remains of creatures transported to their present positions during the biblical Great Deluge. This idea had been proposed as early as the third century by the theologian Tertullian, who pointed out that fossils were crucial evidence of the Deluge.[13] Although references from the early fifteenth century linking fossils to the Deluge are not extant, it may be presumed that this

notion prevailed. For example, less than a century after Van Eyck's painting, Leonardo da Vinci pointed out that his conclusions on the deposition of fossils (which are now considered geologically accurate) countered the widespread view that fossils were tossed into mountainous terrains in one catastrophic flood.[14]

Regardless of the theory favored in the circle of Jan van Eyck, the strategic placement of fossils in the foregrounds of scenery in Early Netherlandish paintings must have caused the viewer to reflect on the origin of such objects. Fossils were considered to be relics and irrefutable evidence of the divinely induced processes of creation and destruction. As such, fossils were imbued with powerful meanings.[15]

Given this viewpoint, the prominently rendered fossils in the *Saint Francis* and other works from the same period (see Appendix) assume special significance. For example, Robert Campin's Mérode altarpiece (fig. 117) and Petrus Christus's *Nativity* (figs. 118, 119) include detailed renderings of fossils. It is possible to match closely the fossil shell morphologies on the stone supporting the uppermost step in Robert Campin's altarpiece to brachiopod fossils (fig. 120). The claw-shaped fossil in the Petrus Christus altarpiece (fig. 121) is a generalized

Fig. 116. Detail of possible lichen growths on a rock in the Philadelphia *Saint Francis*.

Fig. 117. Detail showing fossils in the stone supporting the uppermost step of the left wing of the triptych *The Annunciation* (Mérode altarpiece), by Robert Campin (Flemish, d. 1444), panel, The Metropolitan Museum of Art, The Cloisters Collection, New York, 56.70.

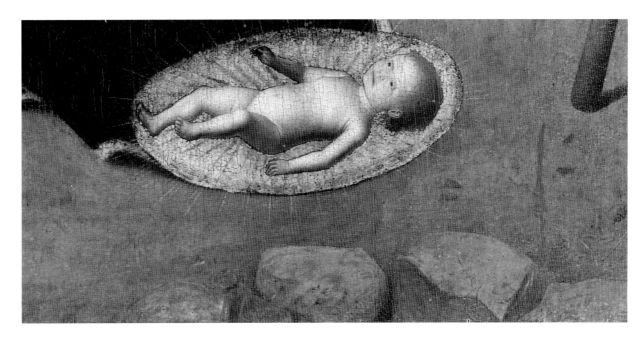

Fig. 118. Detail of *The Nativity*, by Petrus Christus (Netherlandish, 1444–1472/73), panel, National Gallery of Art, Washington, D.C., The Andrew W. Mellon Collection, 1937.1.40.

Fig. 119. Detail of fossils from *The Nativity*, by Petrus Christus (see fig. 118).

Fig. 120. Outline of the stone supporting the uppermost step in the Mérode altarpiece by Robert Campin (see fig. 117).

Fig. 121. Outline of a fossil form in the foreground of *The Nativity* by Petrus Christus (see fig 119).

Fig. 122. Fossil crinoid specimens.

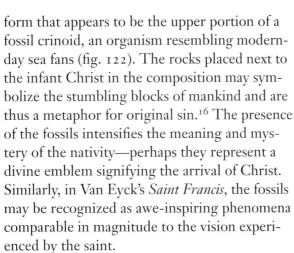

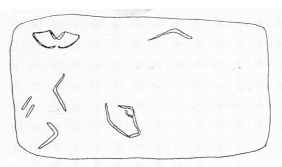

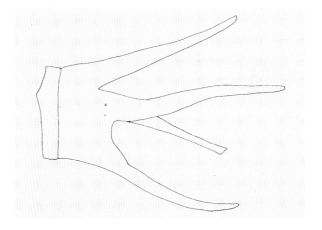

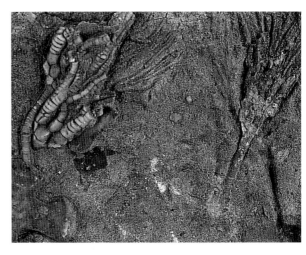

form that appears to be the upper portion of a fossil crinoid, an organism resembling modern-day sea fans (fig. 122). The rocks placed next to the infant Christ in the composition may symbolize the stumbling blocks of mankind and are thus a metaphor for original sin.[16] The presence of the fossils intensifies the meaning and mystery of the nativity—perhaps they represent a divine emblem signifying the arrival of Christ. Similarly, in Van Eyck's *Saint Francis*, the fossils may be recognized as awe-inspiring phenomena comparable in magnitude to the vision experienced by the saint.

The rocks in Van Eyck's *Saint Francis Receiving the Stigmata* reveal the artist's keen interest in observing natural forms, faithfully depicting accurate overall appearance as well as fine and subtle detail. The specific rendering of natural curiosities such as fossil shells as well as contrasting rock morphologies and colors reflects Van Eyck's recognition and celebration of an intricately structured cosmic order created by God. Fossils in such landscapes serve as vivid reminders of the potent forces of creation and catastrophe. Contemplating the mysterious origin of such inanimate phenomena must have been both perplexing and wondrous to the viewer of Van Eyck's landscapes during the fifteenth century.

APPENDIX

Fossils have been observed by the author within the landscapes or architectural stones in the following Netherlandish paintings of the fifteenth and sixteenth centuries:

Robert Campin, *The Annunciation* (Mérode altarpiece), The Metropolitan Museum of Art, The Cloisters Collection, New York (fig. 117).

Rogier van der Weyden, The Three Kings altarpiece, Alte Pinakothek, Munich.

Rogier van der Weyden, Bladelin triptych, Gemäldegalerie, Staatliche Museen zu Berlin Preussischer Kulturbesitz, Berlin.

Jan van Eyck, Ghent altarpiece, St. Bavo's Cathedral, Ghent.

Jan van Eyck, *The Crucifixion* (fig. 21) and *Last Judgment* diptych, The Metropolitan Museum of Art, New York.

After Jan van Eyck, *Calvary*, Galleria Giorgio Franchetti alla Ca' d'Oro, Venice (fig. 91).

Follower of Jan van Eyck, *The Crucifixion*, Gemäldegalerie, Staatliche Museen zu Berlin Preussischer Kulturbesitz, Berlin.

Petrus Christus, *The Nativity*, National Gallery of Art, Washington, D.C. (figs. 118, 119).

Petrus Christus, *Saint Anthony and a Donor*, Staten Museum for Kunst, Copenhagen.

Petrus Christus, *The Crucifixion* (destroyed; see Max J. Friedländer, *Die Van Eyck—Petrus Christus*, vol. 1 of *Die altniederländische Malerei* [Berlin, 1924], pl. 92).

Dierick Bouts, *The Adoration of the Magi* (The Pearl of Brabant triptych), Alte Pinakothek, Munich.

Dierick Bouts, *Joseph and the Two Shepherds*, Musée du Louvre, Paris.

Hugo van der Goes, *The Adoration of the Magi*, Gemäldegalerie, Staatliche Museen zu Berlin Preussischer Kulturbesitz, Berlin.

Hugo van der Goes, *The Adoration of the Shepherds* (Portinari altarpiece), Galleria degli Uffizi, Florence.

Hans Memling, *The Adoration of the Magi* triptych, St. John's Hospital, Memling Museum, Bruges.

Hans Memling, *Panorama of the Epiphanies*, Alte Pinakothek, Munich.

Albert van Ouwater?, *Saint John the Baptist*, Musea de la Capilla Real, Granada.

Fig. 123. Circle of Jan van Eyck, *John the Baptist in a Landscape*, c. 1440s, panel, 15¾ x 5" (40 x 12.5 cm), The Cleveland Museum of Art, Leonard C. Hanna, Jr., Fund, 1979.80.

94

Quentin Massys, *The Rest on the Flight into Egypt*, Worcester Art Museum, Worcester, Massachusetts.

Quentin Massys, *The Crucifixion*, National Gallery of Canada, Ottawa.

Joachim Patinir?, *The Rest on the Flight into Egypt*, Berkshire Museum, Pittsfield, Massachusetts.

Antwerp Mannerist School, *The Adoration of the Magi*, Hyde Collection, Glens Falls, New York.

NOTES

This article is a revised version of a paper presented at the College Art Association 71st Annual Meeting in Philadelphia, February 17–19, 1983.

1. Philadelphia Museum of Art, John G. Johnson Collection, cat. 314 (pl. I). The larger version of this composition at the Galleria Sabauda in Turin (pl. II) shares nearly all the salient features discussed in this article.

2. For example, I completely disagree with the statement of Charles Sterling ("Jan van Eyck avant 1432," *Revue de l'Art*, no. 33 [1976], p. 29) that the limestone cliffs at La Verna are depicted in Van Eyck's painting. Astute descriptions of the new naturalistic quality of rocks painted in works of art of the fifteenth century may be found in E. H. Gombrich, *The Heritage of Apelles: Studies in the Art of the Renaissance* (Ithaca, 1976), pp. 30–34; and in L. B. Gellman, "Petrus Christus," Ph.D. diss., Johns Hopkins University, 1970, p. 114.

3. See John S. Shelton, *Geology Illustrated* (San Francisco, 1966).

4. See Cennino Cennini, *Il Libro dell' arte*, trans. Daniel V. Thompson (New Haven, Conn., 1933), chap. 88. Nearly a century later, Joachim Patinir depicted such rocklike mountain forms in his landscapes.

5. A closely comparable work, *John the Baptist in a Landscape*, Circle of Jan van Eyck, at the Cleveland Museum of Art (fig. 123) has a sedimentary outcrop structurally similar to the one in the Philadelphia painting, but some sections within the strata are tilted unrealistically perpendicular to the overall horizontal layering orientation. The rocks, although roughly identifiable as sandstone and shale, are painted with considerably less detail than in the Philadelphia painting.

6. These marks are not present in the Turin version of this painting.

7. See Arnold H. Bouma, *Sedimentology of Some Flysch Deposits* (Amsterdam, 1962).

8. In their position in the painting, the limestone boulders are not part of the stratified sequence. Unless they are totally unrelated geographically to the strata, we can assume that the strata are also marine in origin.

9. See Sterling, 1976, p. 31.

10. Kenneth Clark proposed that Van Eyck's working method utilized the compilation of outdoor sketches made on the spot (*Landscape into Art* [London, 1949], p. 19).

11. See Archibald Geikie, *The Founders of Geology*, 2nd ed. (New York, 1905); Frank Dawson Adams, *The Birth and Development of the Geological Sciences* (Baltimore, 1938); Edwin Grant, *Physical Science in the Middle Ages* (New York, 1971), esp. p. 18; Henry Faul, *It Began with a Stone: A History of Geology from the Stone Age to the Age of Plate Tectonics* (New York, 1983); Gabriel Gohau, *A History of Geology*, trans. Albert V. Carozzi and Marguerite Carozzi (New Brunswick, N.J., 1991); and David R. Oldroyd, *Thinking about the Earth: A History of Ideas in Geology* (Cambridge, Mass, 1996).

12. See Karl Alfred Ritter von Zittel, *History of Geology and Palaeontology* (New York, 1962); Martin J.S. Rudwick, *The Meaning of Fossils: Episodes in the History of Paleontology* (New York, 1972); and Susan J. Thompson, *A Chronology of Geological Thinking from Antiquity to 1899* (Metuchen, N.J., 1988).

13. See Adams, 1938, p. 254.

14. *The Notebooks of Leonardo da Vinci*, trans. Jean Paul Richter (New York, 1970), vol. 2, pp. 208–18.

15. Adams, 1938, pp. 250–52: "Some regarded them as the works of an occult power or influence at work in nature, perhaps a Spirit or 'Virtu divina' which intended to convey a hidden meaning or lesson, or as being . . . a prophecy of great events to come, set forth in the very rocks of the earth's crust at the time of the creation, ages before the events themselves took place."

16. See J. M. Upton, "Devotional Imagery and Style in the Washington *Nativity* by Petrus Christus," *Studies in the History of Art*, vol. 7 (1977), pp. 48–79.

Katherine Crawford Luber

Annotated Bibliography

A History of the Attributions of the Philadelphia and Turin Versions of "Saint Francis Receiving the Stigmata" by Jan van Eyck

Only those pages that contain specific references to the Philadelphia and Turin paintings are cited.

Waagen, G. F. *Galleries and Cabinets of Art in Great Britain: Being an Account of More than Forty Collections of Paintings, Drawings, Sculptures, Mss., &c. &c., Visited in 1854 and 1856, and Now for the First Time Described*. Vol. 4, supplement to *Treasures of Art in Great Britain, 1854–1857*. London, 1857 (pp. 132, 389).
Waagen reported having seen the painting now in Philadelphia at Heytesbury House. He attributed it to Jan van Eyck, reported the size of the painting as eight by six inches, and surmised that it had been painted at Lisbon in 1428–29.

Pinchart, Alexandre, ed. *Archives des arts, sciences et lettres: Documents inédits*. Vol. 1. Ghent, 1860 (pp. 264–67).
Pinchart first published the text of the 1470 Adornes will as a call to connoisseurs to look for the paintings described therein. He also reproduced the coats of arms of Anselme Adornes and his wife, Marguerite van der Bank, whose portraits were requested to be added to the paintings specified in the will.

Waagen, G. F. *Manuel de l'histoire de la peinture: Ecoles allemande, flamande et hollandaise*. Brussels and Paris, 1863 (p. 102).
Waagen again attributed the Philadelphia painting to Jan van Eyck and argued that it had been painted in Portugal in 1428–29, immediately after the completion of the wings of the Ghent altarpiece.

Crowe, J. A., and G. B. Cavalcaselle. *The Early Flemish Painters: Notices of Their Lives and Works*. 2nd ed. London, 1872 (p. 120).
Noted the existence of *Saint Francis Receiving the Stigmata* in the collection of Lord Heytesbury, although neither of the authors had seen it; they were unaware of the version in Turin.

Crowe, J. A. *Handbook of Painting: The German, Flemish, and Dutch Schools. Based on the Handbook of Kugler Remodelled by the Late Prof. Dr. Waagen*. Rev. ed. London, 1874 (p. 67).
Waagen had attributed the Philadelphia painting to Jan van Eyck and noted that since Lord Heytesbury had acquired it in Lisbon, it was probably painted in Portugal in 1428–29. In a note, Crowe mentioned the Adornes will and suggested that this could be one of the two pictures mentioned, in which case Waagen's suggestion would be incorrect. No mention of the Turin painting.

Wauters, A.-J. *La Peinture flamande*. Paris, 1883 (pp. 52–54).
Wauters compared the landscapes in the two *Saint Francis* paintings to that in the *Virgin of Chancellor Rolin* in the Louvre. He attributed both works to Jan van Eyck late in his career.

Hymans, Henri. "Un tableau retrouvé de Jean van Eyck." *Bulletin des Commissions Royales d'Art et d'Archéologie*, vol. 22 (1883), pp. 108–16.
Hymans attributed the Turin painting to Jan van Eyck but believed it to be in imperfect condition. He did not discuss the Philadelphia painting, although he noted the Adornes will and its mention of two paintings depicting Saint Francis.

Wauters, A.-J. *The Flemish School of Painting*. Trans. Mrs. Henry Rossel. London and Paris, 1885 (pp. 48–50).
Attributed both pictures to Jan van Eyck late in his career and praised the landscapes as being especially fine.

Phillips, Claude. "Correspondance d'Angleterre: Expositions d'hiver de la Royal Academy et de la Grosvenor Gallery à Londres." *La Chronique des Arts et de la Curiosité* (1886), p. 15.
In his review of the winter exhibition of 1886 at the Royal Academy in London, Phillips called the *Saint Francis Receiving the Stigmata* from the collection of Lord Heytesbury (now in Philadelphia) an enigma, and mentioned his doubts about its attribution to Jan van Eyck despite its resemblance to other works by Van Eyck.

[Weale, W. H. James]. "The Royal Academy (First Notice)." *The Athenaeum*, January 9, 1886, p. 73.
Weale noted that Lord Heytesbury had bought the *Saint Francis Receiving the Stigmata* (now in Philadelphia) from a medical man in Lisbon, and attributed it to Jan van Eyck, calling it comparable to the *Virgin of Chancellor Rolin*. He also noted the Adornes will, as well as the existence of another version of the painting in Turin.

Robinson, J. C. "John van Eyck at the Academy Old Masters' Exhibition." *The Times* (London), February 1, 1886, p. 4.
Robinson saw the Philadelphia painting (at that time in the collection of Lord Heytesbury) at the Royal Academy "Old Masters" exhibition of 1886 and accepted its attribution to Jan van Eyck. He then compared it to Antonello da Messina's *Saint Jerome* (now in the National Gallery, London) and suggested that they could have been painted by the same artist. He also noted the presence of the palmettos in the *Saint Francis*, as well as in the *Three Marys at the Sepulchre* (now in Rotterdam), and speculated that the same plants appeared in the Ghent altarpiece. He argued that these plants were evidence of Jan van Eyck's travels in the Iberian peninsula in 1428.

Weale, W. H. James. "John van Eyck at the Academy Old Masters Exhibition." *The Times* (London), February 3, 1886, p. 7.
In a letter written in response to Robinson (see previous entry), Weale noted the existence of a second version of the *Saint Francis* in Turin, connected the two pictures to the Adornes will, and attributed both pictures to Jan van Eyck. However, he noted that the two pictures could not have been painted for Anselme Adornes, since Anselme was only fifteen years old at the time of Jan's death (in fact, he was seventeen). He further argued that both pictures must have been painted in Spain because neither the brown habit of the Franciscans nor the black habit of the Franciscan lay brothers was worn in the Low Countries prior to the end of the fifteenth century.

Weale, W. H. James. "The Royal Academy (Fourth Notice)." *The Athenaeum*, February 6, 1886, p. 208.
Complained that the Heytesbury *Saint Francis* (now in Philadelphia) was hung too low in the Royal Academy show.

Weale, W. H. James. "The Royal Academy (Fifth Notice)." *The Athenaeum*, February 20, 1886, p. 269.
In a scathing response to Robinson's suggestion (see above) that the *Saint Francis* could have been painted by Antonello, Weale again asserted his strong belief in the attribution of the painting to Jan van Eyck. He suggested that the mountain peak depicted in the background could represent Montserrat, and the snow-covered hills, the Pyrenees. He also noted that the face of Saint Francis was clearly a portrait, probably a Spaniard, and that Van Eyck likely made the painting in Spain.

Conway, Martin. *Early Flemish Artists and Their Predecessors on the Lower Rhine*. London, 1887 (p. 141 n. 1).
Conway attributed the Turin painting to Jan van Eyck and called the Philadelphia painting a replica of it. He also mentioned that some scholars believed the Philadelphia painting to be a later copy of the Turin painting.

Dehaisnes, [Chrétien César Auguste]. *Notes sur quelques manuscrits à peintures des maîtres de l'école flamande primitive conservées en Italie: Réunion des Sociétés des Beaux-Arts.* Paris, 1888 (p. 798).
Attributed the Turin painting to Jan van Eyck. No mention of the Philadelphia painting.

Hymans, Henri. "Le Saint François d'Assise de Jean van Eyck." *Gazette des Beaux-Arts*, 2nd period, vol. 37 (1888), pp. 78–83.
Hymans attributed both the Turin and Philadelphia paintings to Jan van Eyck and connected them with the Adornes will. He included heliogravure reproductions of two drawings then in the collection of Count Thierry de Limburg-Stirum and suggested that they might record the portrait wings specified in the Adornes will, and that the wings, now lost, could have been painted by Hans Memling. He also noted that the Philadelphia painting (then in the collection of Lord Heytesbury) had been enlarged, and the surface disfigured by the enlargements.

Jacobsen, Emil. "La Regia Pinacoteca di Torino." *Archivio Storico dell'Arte*, vol. 10 (1897), p. 208.
Called the Turin painting an imitation of a later date and compared its palette to works of Jan Mostaert or Herri met de Bles.

Kaemmerer, Ludwig. *Hubert und Jan van Eyck*. Bielefeld and Leipzig, 1898 (pp. 108–10).
Kaemmerer doubted the attribution of the Turin painting to Jan van Eyck, and on the basis of the comparison of it to the *Saint Anthony* in Copenhagen, suggested that it was painted by Petrus Christus. Since the author had not seen the Philadelphia painting, he withheld judgment on its attribution.

Tschudi, Hugo von. "Jan van Eycks Christus am Kreuz zwischen Maria und Johannes." *Jahrbuch der Königlich Preussischen Kunstsammlungen*, vol. 19 (1898), pp. 202–5.
Tschudi attributed the Turin painting to Jan van Eyck and found its golden tonality comparable to the Berlin *Crucifixion*, which he also attributed to Jan van Eyck. No mention of the Philadelphia painting.

Voll, Karl. *Die Werke des Jan van Eyck: Eine kritische Studie.* Strassburg, 1900 (pp. 109–13).
Voll could see no correspondence to the works of Van Eyck in the Turin picture, despite its quality. He was troubled by its lack of a convincing system of perspective, awkward handling of forms, and poor quality of drawing. He thought the format of the Philadelphia painting (which he knew only from a photograph and with the additions to the sky that made the composition an upright rectangle) suggested that it, like the copy in Madrid, must be a copy after the Turin painting.

Marks, Alfred. "The 'St. Francis' of John van Eyck." *The Athenaeum*, May 26, 1900, pp. 664–65.
To rebut doubts cast on the authenticity of the Turin *Saint Francis*, Marks noted the appearance of the *Chamaerops humilis* (the European fan palm, variously referred to as the "dwarf palm" or "palmetto"), which grows in Portugal and which might have been seen by Jan van Eyck on his journey there in 1428. Marks noted as well that similar vegetation occurs in the Ghent altarpiece and argued that this representation of southern plants assured attribution of both to Jan van Eyck. Marks had not seen the Philadelphia painting (by then in the collection of John G. Johnson) but wondered if the same plants were depicted in it. He also thought that the Philadelphia painting might represent a third example of the composition, since it had been acquired earlier by Lord Heytesbury in Lisbon.

Bode, Wilhelm. "Jan van Eycks Bildnis eines burgundischen Kammerherrn." *Jahrbuch der Königlich Preussischen Kunstsammlungen*, vol. 22 (1901), p. 129.
Bode argued that the Philadelphia painting was a workshop replica of the original in Turin, which he saw as the work of Jan van Eyck. He also argued that the landscape and vegetation could only have been painted by a painter who had himself seen either Spain or Portugal.

Weale, W. H. James. "Hubert van Eyck." *Gazette des Beaux-Arts*, 3rd period, vol. 25 (1901), pp. 474–82.
Weale attributed the Philadelphia painting to Hubert van Eyck, who died in 1426. He believed (incorrectly) that it was in New York and noted the existence of a copy or replica in Turin.

Seeck, Otto. "Die charakteristischen Unterschiede der Brüder Van Eyck." In *Abhandlungen der königlichen Gesellschaft der Wissenschaften zu Göttingen.* Vol. 3. Berlin, 1901 (p. 69).
Seeck attributed the Turin painting to Hubert van Eyck and dated it 1424–26. He made no mention of the Philadelphia painting.

Marks, Alfred. "The Flora of the Van Eycks." *The Athenaeum*, November 1, 1902, p. 593.
Marks argued that Jan (and not Hubert) van Eyck must have painted the landscapes in the paintings that include southern flora. The dwarf palm (*Chamaerops humilis*) appears in four paintings: the Philadelphia and Turin paintings of *Saint Francis*, the *Three Marys at the Sepulchre* (in Rotterdam), and the Copenhagen *Saint Anthony with a Donor* (now commonly attributed to Petrus Christus).

Weale, W. H. James. "The Ghent Altar Piece and the Flora of the Van Eycks." *The Athenaeum*, December 6, 1902.
No mention of either painting.

Marks, Alfred. "The Van Eycks." *The Athenaeum*, December 13, 1902, pp. 800–801.
Attributed the limestone rocks of the Turin *Saint Francis* to Jan van Eyck, within an argument for the continuous collaboration between Hubert and Jan. No mention of the Philadelphia painting.

Phillips, Claude. "Impressions of the Bruges Exhibition." *The Fortnightly Review*, n.s., vol. 72 (1902), p. 596.
Following Weale, Phillips attributed the Philadelphia painting to Hubert van Eyck and noted the existence of the Turin painting, which he believed to be a repetition of lesser quality.

Rosen, Felix. *Die Natur in der Kunst: Studien eines Naturforschers zur Geschichte der Malerei.* Leipzig, 1903 (pp. 105–10, 113).
Rosen, a botanist looking at plant species represented in the works of Van Eyck, argued that the Turin painting must have been painted by Jan van Eyck.

Weale, Frances C. *Hubert and John van Eyck.* London, 1903 (p. 15).
Frances Weale (the daughter of W. H. James Weale) attributed the Philadelphia painting to Hubert van Eyck and wrongly noted that it was in New York. She called the Turin painting a replica with variations and argued that neither work could have been painted in the Low Countries because of the saint's brown habit and the inclusion of the palmetto and other southern shrubs in the landscape.

Durrieu, Paul. "Les Débuts des Van Eyck." *Gazette des Beaux-Arts*, 3rd period, vol. 29 (1903), pp. 9–10.
Durrieu noted that Weale attributed both *Saint Francis* paintings to Hubert van Eyck before 1426.

Weale, W. H. James. "Hubert and John van Eyck." *The Athenaeum*, March 14, 1903, pp. 345–46.
No mention of either painting.

Dvořák, Max. "Das Rätsel der Kunst der Brüder Van Eyck." *Jahrbuch der Kunsthistorischen Sammlungen des Allerhöchsten Kaiserhauses*, vol. 24 (1903), pp. 176, 227–28, 240, 241 n. 1.
Dvořák argued that the Turin painting was a copy after Jan van Eyck's original invention by an artist in the circle of Dierick Bouts or Albert van Ouwater, and that the Philadelphia painting (which he knew only from a photograph) was a sixteenth-century copy after it.

Mont, Pol de. *L'Evolution de la peinture néerlandaise aux XIVe et XVIe siècles et "L'Exposition de Bruges."* Haarlem, [1904] (p. 51).
Although the author had seen neither the Philadelphia nor the Turin painting, he had a photograph of the Turin picture and argued from it that the Turin painting could not be by Jan van Eyck because of the awkward representation

of knees, fantastic representation of the countryside, and idealized expression of the saint himself. He attributed the painting instead to an unknown artist in the immediate vicinity of Jan, although not to Petrus Christus.

Reinach, Salomon. *Apollo: An Illustrated Manual of the History of Art Throughout the Ages*. Trans. Florence Simmonds. New York, 1904 (pp. 220–22).
Reinach noted the history of attribution of the Turin painting to either Hubert or Jan van Eyck. No mention of the Philadelphia painting.

Weale, W. H. James. "Popular Opinions Concerning the Van Eycks." *The Burlington Magazine*, vol. 4 (1904), pp. 35–37.
Weale attributed the Philadelphia painting to Jan van Eyck and wondered if the Turin picture were a later enlargement of the composition by Jan himself or a work by Hubert. He suggested that it would be necessary to see the paintings side by side in order to decide.

Reinach, Salomon. *Répertoire de peintures du moyen âge et de la renaissance (1280–1580)*. 6 vols. Paris, 1905–23 (vol. 1 [1905], p. 681).
Attributed the Turin painting to Jan van Eyck with question; also mentioned the existence of the Philadelphia picture and Weale's recent attribution of it to Hubert van Eyck.

Voll, Karl. *Die altniederländische Malerei von Jan van Eyck bis Memling*. 2 vols. Leipzig, 1906 (vol. 1, pp. 47–48).
Voll knew only the Turin picture, which, on account of the manner of execution of the figures and landscape, he did not believe to be by Jan van Eyck.

Mather, Frank Jewett, Jr. "Recent Additions to the Collection of Mr. John G. Johnson, Philadelphia." *The Burlington Magazine*, vol. 9 (1906), pp. 358–59.
The Philadelphia painting was reproduced for the first time in its smaller format after having been restored by Roger Fry, the founder and editor of *The Burlington Magazine*. Mather noted the close similarities between the Philadelphia and Turin paintings but said that critics had argued that the Philadelphia painting closely resembled those works universally accepted as by Hubert van Eyck.

Ricketts, C. "Pictures in the Collection of Mr. John G. Johnson, of Philadelphia." *The Burlington Magazine*, vol. 9 (1906), p. 426.
Ricketts challenged Mather's attribution of the Philadelphia painting to Hubert van Eyck and called it a later copy of lesser quality after the Turin painting.

Mather, Frank Jewett, Jr. "The Johnson Collection Again." *The Burlington Magazine*, vol. 10 (1906–7), pp. 137–38.
In reply to Ricketts's description of the Philadelphia painting as a "bad, old copy," Mather insisted that the Philadelphia painting was not a copy and was of finer quality than its replica at Turin.

Jaccaci, August F. "Mr. Johnson's Van Eyck." *The Burlington Magazine*, vol. 11 (1907), pp. 46–48.
Entered the Mather-Ricketts debate and cited the two right feet in the Turin version, as well as its general lack of quality, as proof that it was a copy after the painting then in Johnson's possession and now in Philadelphia. Also suggested that the Philadelphia painting should be attributed to Hubert van Eyck because of its sensitive portrayal of spatial depth. Further argued that the Philadelphia painting may have been executed in Italy (thereby explaining the brown habit of Francis) and the Turin painting "in Flanders before the end of the fifteenth century, when the Franciscans there were Greyfriars."

Fourcaud, M. L. de. "La Peinture dans les Pays-Bas et dans le nord de l'Europe." In *Histoire de l'art depuis les premiers temps chrétiens jusqu'à nos jours*. Ed. André Michel. 11 vols. Paris, 1905–29 (vol. 3 [1907], pp. 186–87, 207).
Fourcaud attributed both versions to Jan van Eyck on the basis of style and the Adornes will, and noted as well that both paintings reveal the hand of a miniaturist.

Fierens-Gevaert, [Hippolyte]. *Les Primitifs flamands*. Brussels, 1908 (pp. 11, 14).
Fierens-Gevaert attributed the Turin painting not to Hubert but to Jan van Eyck in the last years of his life. He suggested that Jan had voyaged to Italy and evoked Assisi in the landscape.

Weale, W. H. James. *Hubert and John van Eyck: Their Life and Work*. London and New York, 1908 (pp. 130–35).
Weale cited the Adornes will and based his attribution of both the Turin and Philadelphia paintings to Jan van Eyck on that document. He argued that the brown habit of Francis in the Philadelphia picture provided "conclusive proof" that it was painted in southern Europe, since the first convent of the reformed Franciscans in the Low Countries was founded later in the fifteenth century.

[Brockwell, Maurice W.]. Review of W. H. James Weale, *Hubert and John van Eyck: Their Life and Work* (1908). *The Athenaeum*, April 18, 1908, pp. 484–86.
Argued with Weale's conclusion that the Turin painting was an enlargement of the Philadelphia painting of a later date.

Grant, J. Kirby. "Mr. John G. Johnson's Collection of Pictures in Philadelphia, Part III." *The Connoisseur*, vol. 22 (1908), p. 4.
Attributed the Philadelphia painting to Jan van Eyck and suggested that the figure of Francis was a portrait painted from life. Called the Turin version a replica of the Philadelphia painting by a follower of Jan.

McMahan, Una. "Une exposition documentaire en Pensylvanie [sic]." *Gazette des Beaux-Arts*, 4th period, vol. 1 (1909), p. 182.
Attributed the Philadelphia painting to Hubert van Eyck but made no mention of the Turin painting.

Durand-Gréville, E. *Hubert et Jean van Eyck*. Brussels, 1910 (pp. 110–14, 173).
Durand-Gréville attributed both the Turin and Philadelphia paintings to Hubert van Eyck and dated them to 1416–18, just after the completion of the Turin-Milan Hours. He noted the disparity in the position of the feet in

the two versions, as well as the difference in the representation of the palmetto (*Chamaerops humilis*).

Loo, Georges Hulin de. Introduction to *Heures de Milan: Troisième partie des Très-Belles Heures de Notre-Dame enluminées par les peintures de Jean de France, duc de Berry, et par ceux du duc Guillaume de Bavière, comte du Hainaut et de Hollande*. Brussels and Paris, 1911 (p. 35).
Noted that the foliage types that appear in the two *Saint Francis* paintings and in other works by Jan van Eyck provide proof of his travels to southern Europe.

Weale, W. H. James, and Maurice W. Brockwell. *The Van Eycks and Their Art*. London and New York, 1912 (pp. 93–97, 165–66).
This revised edition of Weale's 1908 monograph noted the difficulty in coming to a clear conclusion about the attribution of the Philadelphia painting to either Hubert or Jan van Eyck based on the following problems: lack of knowledge about Hubert's possible travels; the problematic assumption that the location of the picture in Portugal early in the nineteenth century implied that it had been painted there; the appearance of the brown habit worn by Francis in the Philadelphia painting; and the appearance of the palmetto plant, which suggested that the artist had some familiarity with southern European plants. Weale and Brockwell argued that the stylistic elements and emotion of the picture spoke for an attribution to Hubert, but it could easily be a work by Jan following his brother's manner or copying a drawing by him. They included information about the provenance and the dealer from whom Johnson acquired the picture, and they argued that the Turin picture is a copy of the Philadelphia painting.

Valentiner, W. R. *Flemish and Dutch Paintings*. Vol. 2 of *Catalogue of a Collection of Paintings and Some Art Objects*. Philadelphia, 1913 (pp. 3–4).
In this catalogue of the Johnson collection, Valentiner noted that Weale had attributed both the Philadelphia and Turin paintings to Jan van Eyck and that the Philadelphia version was the first one painted. He listed other opinions but concluded that the Philadelphia painting was an authentic work by Jan van Eyck.

Fürbringer, Hermann. *Die künstlerischen Voraussetzungen des Genter Altars der Brüder Van Eyck*. Weida, 1914 (p. 94).
Fürbringer noted the much-contested attribution of the Turin painting, even though he had not seen it. He compared it to the landscape in the *Madonna with the Carthusian* in the Frick Collection, New York, which he felt was too good to be by Petrus Christus but which was not by Van Eyck. He also noted the similarities in the rocky landscape of the *Saint Francis* paintings to the landscape in the Ghent altarpiece.

Friedländer, Max J. "Jan van Eyck." In *Allgemeines Lexikon der bildenden Künstler von der Antike bis zur Gegenwart*. Comp. Ulrich Thieme and Felix Becker. 37 vols. Leipzig, 1907–50 (vol. 11 [1915], p. 131).
Included both versions as autograph works by Jan van Eyck but gave primacy to the Turin painting in terms of chronology.

Friedländer, Max J. *Von Eyck bis Bruegel: Studien zur Geschichte der niederländischen Malerei*. Berlin, 1916 (p. 183 and pl. 1).
Attributed both the Turin and Philadelphia paintings to Jan van Eyck late in his career, around 1438.

Winkler, Friedrich. "Über verschollene Bilder der Brüder Van Eyck." *Jahrbuch der Königlich Preussischen Kunstsammlungen*, vol. 37 (1916), p. 288.
Noted the similarity in rock formations in Eyckian pictures, including the Ghent altarpiece, the Turin and Philadelphia paintings, the *Christ in the Garden of Gethsemane* miniature in the Turin-Milan Hours, and the *Bearing of the Cross* in Budapest, without making a strong argument about specific attributions.

Mather, Frank Jewett, Jr.. "The John G. Johnson Collection." *American Magazine of Art*, vol. 8 (1916–17), p. 341.
Attributed the Philadelphia painting to Jan van Eyck. No mention of the Turin painting.

Conway, Martin. *The Van Eycks and Their Followers*. London, 1921 (p. 60).
Conway attributed the Philadelphia painting to Hubert van Eyck and called the Turin painting a repetition of it. He noted the existence of the Adornes will and postulated the possible connection to the two paintings.

Brockwell, Maurice W. "The Ince-Blundell Van Eyck." *Art in America*, vol. 11 (1923), p. 149.
Called the Philadelphia painting the "only universally accepted painting by either of the Van Eycks on the Continent of America." No mention of the Turin painting.

Goffin, Arnold. *L'Art religieux en Belgique: La Peinture des origines à la fin du XVIIIme siècle*. Brussels and Paris, 1924 (p. 32).
Mentioned the existence of three versions (in Philadelphia, Turin, and Madrid) and noted Georges Hulin de Loo's assertion that the Turin version is the original.

Winkler, Friedrich. *Die altniederländische Malerei: Die Malerei in Belgien und Holland von 1400–1600*. Berlin, 1924 (p. 64).
Attributed both the Turin and Philadelphia paintings to Jan van Eyck and compared the space and naturalism achieved in them to the Antwerp *Saint Barbara*.

Friedländer, Max J. *Die Van Eyck–Petrus Christus*. Vol. 1 of *Die altniederländische Malerei*. Berlin, 1924 (pp. 101–4).
Friedländer saw both paintings as autograph works of Jan van Eyck, either copying his own work or producing both paintings after a single preparatory drawing. He rejected arguments that either or both paintings were made in Portugal (and therefore about 1429), since the Adornes will placed both pictures in Bruges in 1470. He dated both to the end of Van Eyck's career, about 1438. He also described the known provenance of the two pictures, noting that the Turin painting was in the possession of a nun in Casale Monferrato in the early nineteenth century and that the Philadelphia painting was acquired in Lisbon in 1830.

Dvořák, Max. *Das Rätsel der Kunst der Brüder Van Eyck.* Munich, 1925 (p. 124 n. 3).
On the basis of a photograph, Dvořák argued that the Philadelphia picture is a sixteenth-century copy of the Turin picture, which he attributed to Hubert van Eyck.

Devigne, Marguerite. *Van Eyck.* Brussels and Paris, 1926 (pp. 121–23).
Devigne attributed the Philadelphia painting to Jan van Eyck and dated it to about 1438; she believed the Turin painting to be a copy but connected both paintings to the Adornes will.

Heyse, Albert. "Un primitif flamand de la collection de Mr. Amédée Prouvost de Roubaix." *Gand Artistique,* vol. 5 (1926), pp. 222–23.
Argued that the Turin painting is a late sixteenth-century work.

Mayer, August L. "A Jan van Eyck Problem." *The Burlington Magazine,* vol. 48 (1926), p. 200.
Mayer argued that the Philadelphia painting should be attributed to Jan van Eyck and that it was completely different in technique and superior to the version in Turin, which appeared to be a copy by a painter active at least a generation after Jan. He was not convinced that the pair should be associated with the Adornes will and argued that the depiction of southern flora, together with the purchase of the picture in Portugal, suggested an early date of about 1429.

Bodkin, Thomas. Letter to the Editor. *The Burlington Magazine,* vol. 48 (1926), pp. 273–74.
Based on the problematic representation of Brother Leo's left foot in the Turin painting, Bodkin argued that the Philadelphia painting must be a work by Hubert van Eyck. He posed his observation as a query to Roger Fry about the cleaning of the Philadelphia painting and questioned whether or not Fry had observed anything during the cleaning that would have led the copyist in the Turin picture to misrepresent the foot in this way.

Fry, Roger. Editorial letter. *The Burlington Magazine,* vol. 48 (1926), p. 274.
In his response to Thomas Bodkin (see previous entry), Fry discussed his cleaning of the Philadelphia painting after its acquisition by Johnson. He said that he removed an addition in the area of the sky along with numerous overpaints, revealing the good state of preservation of the painting as well as the red border. Relying on the misunderstood left foot of Brother Leo in the Turin painting, Fry argued that the Philadelphia painting must be a work by Hubert van Eyck and that the Turin version is a copy.

Fierens-Gevaert, [Hippolyte]. *Histoire de la peinture flamande des origines à la fin du XVe siècle.* 3 vols. Paris, 1927–29 (vol. 1 [1927], p. 102).
Although he had not seen the Philadelphia picture, Fierens-Gevaert argued that Jan van Eyck painted both versions.

Sperling, Harry G. *Catalogue of Loan Exhibition of Flemish Primitives in Aid of the Free Milk Fund for Babies, Inc.* Exh. cat. New York, 1929 (pp. 14, 22–23).
In this catalogue for the exhibition at the Kleinberger Galleries, New York, Sperling attributed both the Philadelphia and Turin paintings to Jan van Eyck and associated them with the Adornes will. Sperling suggested that the piece of sky removed from the picture by Roger Fry was original, and he provided evidence that the painting was originally the central panel of a triptych.

"Flemish Show Opens Today at Kleinberger's: Paintings of the XVth and XVIth Centuries, from Van Eyck to Van Orley, Loaned from Many Public and Private Collections." *The Art News,* vol. 28, no. 4 (October 26, 1929), p. 4.
The Philadelphia painting was included in the exhibition at Kleinberger Galleries as a work of Jan van Eyck and was said to illustrate both the "amazing control of detail" and "the ability to subordinate minutiae to mass" that characterized Jan's work. No mention of the Turin painting.

Goodrich, Lloyd. "Exhibitions: The Kleinberger Galleries." *The Arts,* vol. 16 (1929), pp. 174–76.
In his review of the exhibition at the Kleinberger Galleries, Goodrich mentioned the Philadelphia painting and attributed it to Jan van Eyck.

Vaughan, Malcolm. "A Loan Exhibition of Flemish Primitives." *International Studio,* vol. 94, no. 390 (November 1929), p. 38.
Vaughan described the Philadelphia painting as the only work by the Van Eycks in America. No mention of the Turin painting.

[Goldschmidt, Daisy]. *Exposition internationale coloniale, maritime et d'art flamand: Section d'art flamand ancien.* 4 vols. Antwerp, 1930 (vol. 1, p. 50, no. 132).
Attributed both the Turin and Philadelphia paintings to Jan van Eyck and suggested that the figure of Saint Francis was a portrait of Anselme Adornes's father.

Fierens, Paul. *Jean van Eyck.* Paris, 1931 (pp. 22–23).
Attributed both the Philadelphia and Turin paintings to Jan van Eyck and connected them to the Adornes will.

De Poorter, A. "Testament van Anselmus Adornes, 10 Febr. 1470." *Biekorf* (Bruges), vol. 37 (1931), pp. 225–39.
Reproduced the Adornes will and the description therein of two portraits of Saint Francis by the hand of Jan van Eyck to be bequeathed to his two daughters.

Pacchioni, Guglielmo. *La Regia Pinacoteca di Torino.* Vol. 16 of *Itinerari dei musei e monumenti d'Italia.* Rome, 1932 (p. 9).
Attributed both the Turin and Philadelphia paintings to Jan van Eyck.

Puyvelde, Leo van. "Jean van Eyck: Saint François recevant les stigmates." In *Trésor de l'art flamand du moyen âge au XVIIIme siècle: Mémorial de l'exposition d'art flamand ancien à Anvers 1930 par un groupe de spécialistes.* 2 vols. Antwerp, 1932 (vol. 1, pp. 29–30).
Attributed both the Philadelphia and Turin paintings to Jan van Eyck and believed that the error in the representa-

tion of Brother Leo's feet had been made by Van Eyck himself.

Post, Chandler Rathfon. *A History of Spanish Painting*. 14 vols. Cambridge, Mass., 1930–66 (vol. 4 [1933], pp. 20–21).
Post attributed both versions to Jan van Eyck but argued that there was insufficient evidence to suggest that either version had been painted on the Iberian peninsula. Even though the landscape, vegetation, and brown habit of Francis suggest a knowledge of Spain, Post argued that Van Eyck could have painted these features from memory at a later date.

Clysters, L. *Kunst en mystiek: De aanbidding van het Lam: Naar een genetische verklaring*. Tongerloo, 1935 (pp. 200–201).
Noted the existence of the Adornes will and associated both the Philadelphia and Turin paintings with the two paintings mentioned there.

Hoogewerff, G. J. *Vlaamsche kunst en Italiaansche renaissance*. Antwerp, 1935 (pp. 23–25).
Hoogewerff mentioned the Adornes will, attributed the Philadelphia painting to Jan van Eyck, and noted that the head of Saint Francis in that painting was very portraitlike. In contrast, he believed the figure of Francis in the Turin painting to be less portraitlike and found that the larger composition size suggested that it was by a follower who knew the Philadelphia painting, possibly Petrus Christus.

Renders, Emile. *Jean van Eyck*. Bruges, 1935 (pp. 75–83).
Attributed the Philadelphia painting to Jan van Eyck, dated it to around 1430, and called the Turin painting a copy. Noted the close correspondences between the Philadelphia *Saint Francis* and the Rotterdam *Three Marys at the Sepulchre*.

Tietze, Hans, ed. *Meisterwerke europäischer Malerei in Amerika*. Vienna, 1935 (pp. 120, 332).
Attributed the Philadelphia painting to Jan van Eyck, while noting the dispute of attribution in the literature. Also noted the existence of a second version in Turin.

Lavalleye, Jacques. "De Vlaamsche schilderkunst tot ongeveer 1480." In *Geschiedenis van de Vlaamsche kunst*. Ed. Stan Leurs. Antwerp, 1936 (pp. 178–79).
Lavalleye attributed the Philadelphia painting to Jan van Eyck, called the Turin painting a replica, and noted that some scholars had attributed it to Petrus Christus.

Friedländer, Max J. "Über den Zwang der ikonographischen Tradition in der vlämischen Kunst." *The Art Quarterly*, vol. 1 (1938), p. 20.
In this discussion of replicas made by artists, Friedländer mentioned the Turin and Philadelphia paintings as examples of Van Eyck himself making replicas of his own compositions.

De Tolnay, Charles. *Le Maître de Flémalle et les frères Van Eyck*. Brussels, 1939 (pp. 33–34, 68).
De Tolnay argued that the Philadelphia painting was made by Jan van Eyck late in his career, about 1438–39.

Worcester Art Museum and the John G. Johnson Collection. *The Worcester-Philadelphia Exhibition of Flemish Painting*. Exh. cat. Worcester and Philadelphia, 1939 (pp. 15–17).
The Philadelphia *Saint Francis* was attributed to Jan van Eyck, as was the Turin painting. The Adornes will be mentioned along with the possibility that these two paintings are the ones mentioned therein.

Beenken, Hermann. *Hubert und Jan van Eyck*. Munich, 1941 (pp. 31–33).
Beenken considered the Philadelphia version to be the original of the two works, painted about 1426–29, and the Turin version an autograph replica of a slightly later date. He also argued that the Philadelphia *Saint Francis* must have been painted in Portugal because of the examples of southern flora included in the landscape.

[Marceau, Henri]. *John G. Johnson Collection: Catalogue of Paintings*. Philadelphia, 1941 (p. 27).
Attributed both the Philadelphia and Turin paintings to Jan van Eyck and connected them to the Adornes will.

Beenken, Hermann. "Jan van Eyck und die Landschaft: Zur 500 Jährigen Wiederkehr von Jans Todestag im Juli 1441." *Pantheon*, vol. 28 (1941), pp. 173–78.
Attributed the Philadelphia painting to Jan van Eyck. No mention of the Turin painting.

Palazzo Strozzi, Florence. *Catalogo della mostra d'arte fiamminga e olandese dei secoli XV e XVI*. Exh. cat. Florence, 1948 (p. 5, no. 1).
The Turin painting was described as one of the principal works of Jan van Eyck. The Italian provenance of the painting was noted, as well as the existence of a second version by the same hand in Philadelphia.

Kimball, Fiske, and Lionello Venturi. *Great Paintings in America*. New York, 1948 (p. 62).
Attributed both the Philadelphia and Turin paintings to Jan van Eyck and connected them to the Adornes will.

Musper, [Heinrich] Theodor. *Untersuchungen zu Rogier van der Weyden und Jan van Eyck*. Stuttgart, [1948] (pp. 95, 103, 107).
Attributed the Philadelphia painting to Jan van Eyck and dated it about 1430–32. The painting in Turin was described as softer, even if painted by the same hand.

Puyvelde, Leo van. *The Flemish Primitives*. Trans. D. I. Wilton. Brussels, 1948 (p. 25).
Puyvelde attributed the Philadelphia painting to Jan van Eyck on stylistic grounds but made no mention of the Turin painting.

Devigne, Marguerite. "L'Art aux États-Unis: Les Musées." *Revue Générale Belge*, no. 38 (December 1948), pp. 229–35.
Devigne attributed the Philadelphia and Turin paintings to Jan van Eyck but mistakenly noted that the Philadelphia painting was larger than the one in Turin. She corrected her error in a note in a subsequent issue of the same journal (no. 42 [April 1949], p. 869 n. 1).

Bertram, Anthony. *The Van Eycks: Hubert and Jan*. London and New York, 1950 ([p. 58], pl. 43).
Attributed the Philadelphia painting to Jan van Eyck but made no mention of the Turin painting.

Renders, Emile. *Jean van Eyck et le polyptyque: Deux problèmes résolus*. 3 vols. Brussels, 1950 (vol. 1, pp. 89–91).
Attributed the Philadelphia painting to Jan van Eyck but made no mention of the Turin painting.

Baldass, Ludwig. "The Ghent Altarpiece of Hubert and Jan van Eyck." *The Art Quarterly*, vol. 13 (1950), p. 190 and n. 14.
Baldass knew the Philadelphia painting only through a photograph but argued that it was painted by Jan van Eyck while still under the influence of Hubert, before Jan's commission to complete the Ghent altarpiece. He thought the Turin painting was "painted in a dry and lifeless manner, coarse in spots," and not by Jan van Eyck.

[Bernardi, Marziano]. *Ventiquattro capolavori della Galleria Sabauda di Torino*. Turin, 1951 (pp. 50–51).
Attributed both the Turin and Philadelphia paintings to Jan van Eyck.

Sulzberger, S[uzanne]. "Une particularité du paysage eyckien." *Scriptorium*, vol. 5 (1951), p. 43.
Sulzberger argued that Jan van Eyck reclaimed the use of the horizon line in his depiction of space from the painters of the antique. She included in the group of works with this exceptional compositional development the *Prayer on the Shore* or *Arrival of a Count of Holland* page from the Turin–Milan Hours (Turin folio 59 verso; destroyed), the *Crucifixion* and *Last Judgment* diptych in the Metropolitan Museum of Art, the Philadelphia and Turin paintings of *Saint Francis*, and the *Virgin of Chancellor Rolin* in the Louvre, and attributed them all, by implication, to Jan van Eyck.

Bazin, Germain. "Petrus Christus et les rapports entre l'Italie et la Flandre au milieu du XVᵉ siècle." *La Revue des Arts*, vol. 4 (1952), p. 204 n. 44.
Attributed both versions to Jan van Eyck.

Aru, C., and E. de Geradon. *La Galerie Sabauda de Turin*. Vol. 5 of *Les Primitifs flamands: 1. Corpus de la peinture des anciens Pays-Bas méridionaux au quinzième siècle*. Antwerp, 1952 (pp. 5–13).
Attributed both the Turin and Philadelphia paintings to Jan van Eyck.

Baldass, Ludwig. *Jan van Eyck*. New York and London, 1952 (pp. 30, 44, 276–77).
Baldass dated the Philadelphia painting early in Jan's career, to about 1425. He also noted the experimental quality of the Philadelphia painting, discernible in the faulty proportions of the figures of Francis and Leo. He argued that the structure of the landscape and individual elements within it were similar to those of Hubert, but more firmly based on Jan's close observation of nature. He regarded the Turin painting as the work of a copyist who had misunderstood the original form of the Philadelphia painting.

Pächt, Otto. "The Literature of Art: A New Book on the Van Eycks." *The Burlington Magazine*, vol. 95 (1953), p. 253 n. 15.
In this review of Baldass's *Jan van Eyck*, Pächt noted the close stylistic relationship between the Turin *Saint Francis* and Hubert's part of the Ghent altarpiece. He agreed with Baldass's early dating of the two pictures as more convincing than the late dating of De Tolnay, Puyvelde, and Friedländer. Pächt also argued that the Adornes will pointed misleadingly to Jan van Eyck as the author of both paintings.

Panofsky, Erwin. *Early Netherlandish Painting: Its Origins and Character*. 2 vols. Cambridge, Mass., 1953 (vol. 1, pp. 192 n. 1, 300, 312, 432).
Panofsky argued that both the Philadelphia and Turin paintings were conglomerations of Eyckian motifs and that the attributions to Jan were based largely on the Adornes will, which he found problematic in structure. He also suggested that Petrus Christus might have painted both versions.

Brockwell, Maurice W. *The Van Eyck Problem*. London, 1954 (pp. 53, 59–62).
Brockwell rejected Weale's attribution of the Philadelphia painting to Hubert van Eyck and attributed it instead to Jan van Eyck. No mention of the Turin painting.

Denis, Valentin. *Tutta la pittura di Jan van Eyck*. Milan, 1954 (pp. 32, 36–37, 54).
Argued that the Philadelphia painting was by Jan van Eyck, about 1430, but that the Turin version was a later copy.

Genaille, Robert. *Flemish Painting from Van Eyck to Brueghel*. Trans. Leslie Schenk. New York, 1954 (p. 132).
Attributed both the Philadelphia and Turin paintings to Jan van Eyck's latest period, around 1438.

Meiss, Millard. Review of Erwin Panofsky, *Early Netherlandish Painting: Its Origins and Character* (1953). *The New York Times*, March 7, 1954.
Agreed with Panofsky's assessment that the Philadelphia version was not painted by Jan van Eyck.

Held, Julius S. Review of Erwin Panofsky, *Early Netherlandish Painting: Its Origins and Character* (1953). *The Art Bulletin*, vol. 37 (1955), p. 218.
In opposition to Panofsky, Held argued that the Turin version was superior to the Philadelphia painting and that it "might be, or might reflect" an early painting by Jan van Eyck.

Pächt, Otto. "Panofsky's 'Early Netherlandish Painting.'" *The Burlington Magazine*, vol. 98 (1956), pp. 110–16, 267–79.
No mention of either painting.

Weiss, Roberto. "Jan van Eyck and the Italians, I: The Merchants." *Italian Studies*, vol. 11 (1956), p. 6.
Weiss mentioned the Adornes will as well as the existence of the paintings in Philadelphia and Turin, which he called Eyckian. He argued that there is no evidence beyond the subject matter to connect the two paintings to the will, and added in a note that Panofsky had doubted the attribution of either to Jan van Eyck.

Bruyn, Josua. *Van Eyck Problemen: De Levensbron, het werk van een leerling van Jan van Eyck*. Utrecht, 1957 (p. 99 n. 1).
Bruyn knew the Philadelphia painting only through reproductions but mentioned that Baldass had called it the stronger of the two versions. He saw in the Turin painting a late work of Jan van Eyck with perhaps some work completed by an assistant. He also stated that Panofsky's doubts about the attribution of either painting to Jan van Eyck were completely unfounded.

Châtelet, Albert. "Les Enluminures eyckiennes des manuscrits de Turin et de Milan-Turin." *La Revue des Arts*, vol. 7 (1957), pp. 155–64.
Châtelet identified Jean Coene of Bruges as Hand H of the Turin Hours and argued that he also painted the *Crucifixion* and *Last Judgment* diptych in the Metropolitan Museum of Art, the *Crucifixion* in the Ca' d'Oro in Venice, the Detroit *Saint Jerome*, as well as the Philadelphia *Saint Francis*.

Lassaigne, Jacques. *Flemish Painting: The Century of Van Eyck*. Trans. Stuart Gilbert. Geneva, 1957 (p. 60).
Lassaigne saw both the Philadelphia and Turin pictures as Eyckian in character and dated them to the early 1420s.

Fierens, Paul. *La Peinture flamande: Des origines à Quentin Metsys*. Paris, 1958 (pp. 22–23).
Fierens attributed both the Philadelphia and Turin paintings to Jan van Eyck and noted that despite the multiple connections between Italy and Bruges, Jan did not seem to have traveled south of the Alps. He argued, therefore, that the landscapes in both the Philadelphia and Turin paintings are imaginary or at least invented.

Salvini, Roberto. *La pittura fiamminga*. Milan, 1958 (p. 44).
Following Panofsky, Salvini suggested both versions were painted by a follower of Jan van Eyck.

Desneux, Jules. "Underdrawings and *Pentimenti* in the Pictures of Jan van Eyck." *The Art Bulletin*, vol. 40 (1958), pp. 13–21.
No mention of either painting.

Puyvelde, Leo van. *Les Primitifs flamands*. Brussels, 1959 (pp. 61, 88).
Attributed the Philadelphia painting to Jan van Eyck but made no mention of the Turin painting.

Denis, Valentin. *All the Paintings of Jan van Eyck*. Trans. Paul Colacicchi. London, 1961 (pp. 27, 37–38).
Denis found the Philadelphia *Saint Francis* comparable in technique to the *Adoration of the Mystic Lamb* and suggested that the version in Turin was a copy of the Philadelphia painting.

Bruyn, Josua. "Twee kardinaalsportretten in het werk van Jan van Eyck." In *Album discipulorum aangeboden aan Prof. J. G. van Gelder*. Utrecht, 1963 (pp. 28–30).
Bruyn argued that the Philadelphia version is undoubtedly by Jan van Eyck and that the Turin version is "mostly" by his hand, although he saw the two as quite different in style. He saw the Philadelphia painting as close in style to the late Dresden triptych of 1437 and the *Madonna by the Fountain* of 1439. The Turin version is, according to Bruyn, closer in style to the *Saint Jerome* in Detroit. He noted correspondences between the crucifix in the *Saint Francis* paintings and the Detroit *Saint Jerome*.

Folie, Jacqueline. "Les Oeuvres authentifiées des primitifs flamands." *Bulletin of the IRPA-KIK (Institut Royal du Patrimoine Artistique Koninklijk Institut voor het Kunstpatrimonium)*, vol. 6 (1963), p. 202.
Folie argued that neither version should be included among authenticated works of Jan van Eyck.

Denis, Valentin. *The Adoration of the Mystic Lamb*. Trans. Michael Langley. Milan, 1964 (p. 43).
Denis attributed the Philadelphia painting to Jan van Eyck, dated it from about 1430, and argued that Francis must be a portrait of Francesco Adornes, whom he believed (incorrectly) to be the father of Anselme Adornes.

[Dohmann, Albrecht]. *Die altniederländische Malerei des fünfzehnten Jahrhunderts von Van Eyck bis Bosch*. Leipzig, 1964 (p. 28).
Dohmann noted the Adornes will, mentioned the Philadelphia and Turin paintings, and argued that the quality of the Philadelphia painting seemed higher than that of the one in Turin. He argued that the painting must date from relatively early in Van Eyck's career, given the striking correspondences between the Philadelphia *Saint Francis* and the *Christ in the Garden of Gethsemane* from the Turin-Milan Hours. He noted that the rocks in the foreground are very reminiscent of the middle panel of the Ghent altarpiece, and concluded that it will remain unknown whether Jan van Eyck himself repeated the composition or whether he had someone in his workshop repeat it for him.

Friedländer, Max J. *The Van Eycks–Petrus Christus*. Trans. Heinz Norden. Vol. 1 of *Early Netherlandish Painting*. Leiden and Brussels, 1967 (pp. 62–63).
This English edition of Friedländer's 1924 work added nothing and changed nothing about the attribution and dating of the two pictures, both of which remained attributed to Jan van Eyck and dated late in his career, to about 1438.

Châtelet, Albert. Introduction to *Heures de Turin: Quarante-cinq feuillets à peintures provenant des Très Belles Heures de Jean de France, duc de Berry*. Turin, 1967 (p. xviii).
In this revised edition of the 1902 facsimile edition, Châtelet attributed the Philadelphia *Saint Francis* to Hand H of the Turin Hours, whom he identified as the artist Jean Coene. He also attributed the *Last Judgment* diptych in the Metropolitan Museum of Art, the *Crucifixion* in the Ca' d'Oro in Venice, and the Detroit *Saint Jerome* to Jean Coene.

Marrow, James. Review of the revised edition of *Heures de Turin* (1967). *The Art Bulletin*, vol. 50 (1968), pp. 203–9.
Marrow contested Châtelet's grouping of the Eyckian paintings—which included the Philadelphia *Saint Francis* but not the Turin one—with Hand H of the Turin-Milan Hours.

Cuttler, Charles D. *Northern Painting from Pucelle to Bruegel: Fourteenth, Fifteenth, and Sixteenth Centuries*. New York, 1968 (p. 103).

Cuttler argued that both the Philadelphia and Turin paintings are replicas of a lost work by Jan van Eyck.

Puyvelde, Leo van. *Flemish Painting from the Van Eycks to Metsys*. Trans. Alan Kendall. London, 1968 (pp. 12, 57).
Attributed the Philadelphia painting to Jan van Eyck.

Faggin, Giorgio T. *L'opera completa dei Van Eyck*. Intro. by Raffaello Brignetti. Milan, 1968 (p. 89).
Faggin attributed the Philadelphia painting to Jan van Eyck and the Turin painting to a Flemish follower of about 1450.

Faggin, Giorgio T. *The Complete Paintings of the Van Eycks*. Intro. by Robert Hughes. New York, [1968] (pp. 88–89).
Faggin noted the existence of the Adornes will but pointed out that there are problems of authenticity, both with the will and with the composition of the Philadelphia and Turin paintings. If the two pictures are indeed autograph, they would have to be dated early in Jan's career, about the same time as the Berlin *Virgin in the Church*.

Faggin, Giorgio T. *Tout l'oeuvre peint des frères Van Eyck*. Intro. by Albert Châtelet. Paris, 1969 (p. 89).
The Philadelphia painting was attributed to Jan with doubts; the Turin painting was identified as a slightly later Flemish copy executed around 1450.

Peman y Pemartin, Cesar. *Juan van Eyck y España*. Cadiz, 1969 (pp. 46–48).
Cited Baldass's views that both the Philadelphia and Turin paintings are early works by Jan van Eyck.

Mazzini, Franco. *Turin: The Sabauda Gallery*. Turin, 1969 (p. xv).
Attributed the Turin painting to Jan van Eyck.

Philip, Lotte Brand. *The Ghent Altarpiece and the Art of Jan van Eyck*. Princeton, 1971 (p. 127 n. 250).
Philip argued that any doubts about Jan van Eyck's authorship of the *Saint Francis* (based on Panofsky's objections about the spatial construction of the composition) should be dispelled.

[Sweeny, Barbara]. *John G. Johnson Collection: Catalogue of Flemish and Dutch Paintings*. Philadelphia, 1972 (pp. 35–37).
Attributed both the Philadelphia and Turin paintings to Jan van Eyck.

Philadelphia Museum of Art. *Treasures of the Philadelphia Museum of Art and the John G. Johnson Collection*. Philadelphia, 1973 (p. 34).
Attributed the Philadelphia painting to Jan van Eyck; no mention of the Turin painting.

Snyder, James. "The Chronology of Jan van Eyck's Paintings." In *Album amicorum J. G. van Gelder*. The Hague, 1973 (pp. 296 n. 16, 297).
Attributed the Philadelphia *Saint Francis* to Jan van Eyck late in his career (c. 1438–39) and compared the figure of Saint Francis to the kneeling donor in the Dresden triptych. Made no mention of the Turin painting.

Schabacker, Peter H. *Petrus Christus*. Utrecht, 1974 (pp. 52 n. 3, 112).
Schabacker doubted the attribution of either the Philadelphia or the Turin painting to Jan van Eyck; however, he saw no relationship to Petrus Christus either. He called both versions Eyckian and noted that they have been related to Italy by virtue of their mention in the Adornes will.

Panhans, Günter. "Florentiner Maler verarbeiten ein eyckisches Bild." *Wiener Jahrbuch für Kunstgeschichte*, vol. 27 (1974), pp. 196–97 and n. 31.
Concluded that the Turin version is by Hubert van Eyck and the Philadelphia version is a copy by Jan van Eyck.

Gombrich, E. H. "Light, Form and Texture in Fifteenth-Century Painting North and South of the Alps." In *The Heritage of Apelles: Studies in the Art of the Renaissance*. Ithaca, 1976 (pp. 33–34).
Attributed the Philadelphia painting to Jan van Eyck; no mention of the Turin painting.

Sterling, Charles. "Jan van Eyck avant 1432." *Revue de l'Art*, no. 33 (1976), pp. 29–30, 56, 101.
Accepted the Turin *Saint Francis* as an autograph work of Jan van Eyck and argued that the Philadelphia painting was a copy after it.

[Kuroe, Mitsuhiko]. *Van Eyck*. Vol. 2 of *L'Art du monde*. Tokyo, 1978 (p. 109).
Kuroe referred to Weale's publications of 1908 and 1912 and noted the existence of the Adornes will with its mention of two portraits of Saint Francis by Jan van Eyck. After making reference to the most significant art-historical literature, Kuroe argued for an attribution of the Philadelphia painting to Jan van Eyck before the completion of the Ghent altarpiece, about 1428–29; he saw the Turin painting as an old copy after the Philadelphia painting. [I wish to thank Sumiko Imai for her assistance with the translation of this book. *KCL*]

Trost, Edit. *Jan van Eyck*. Berlin, 1978 (p. 10).
Trost mentioned that a *Saint Francis* belongs to the group of small paintings (like the *Madonna in a Church*, and the *Annunciation* in Washington, D.C.) that preceded the Ghent altarpiece. However, Trost did not identify which of the two *Saint Francis* paintings she meant.

Dhanens, Elisabeth. *Hubert and Jan van Eyck*. Antwerp, 1980 (pp. 363–66).
Dhanens argued that Jan van Eyck never copied himself. Her attributions of paintings to the artist or to followers were based on the degree of dependence on the Ghent altarpiece; therefore, neither the Turin nor the Philadelphia painting is included in her catalogue of authentic Eyckian works. Dhanens also compared the landscape in the two *Saint Francis* paintings to the Copenhagen *Saint Anthony* and noted that the boat with its reflection in the water was a motif frequently copied by Eyckian followers.

Paolini, Maria Grazia. "Problemi antonelliani—I rapporti con la pittura fiamminga." *Storia dell'Arte*, nos. 38–40 (1980), pp. 160–61.

Paolini noted the existence of two almost identical versions and saw both the Philadelphia and Turin paintings as copies by Petrus Christus after an Eyckian invention.

Châtelet, Albert. *Early Dutch Painting: Painting in the Northern Netherlands in the Fifteenth Century*. Trans. Christopher Brown and Anthony Turner. Amsterdam, 1981 (pp. 42–43, 200–201).
Châtelet attributed the Philadelphia painting to Master H of the Turin-Milan Hours because of the miniature-like quality of the composition. He remarked that the surface of the Turin painting made its quality difficult to assess, although he doubted it could be a work by Jan van Eyck. Châtelet theorized that Master H inherited Van Eyck's workshop and would have had a prototype "pattern" for the composition in his possession after the death of Van Eyck. Therefore the two paintings of *Saint Francis* could be those mentioned in the Adornes will without actually being by Jan van Eyck.

Lurie, Ann Tzeutschler. "A Newly Discovered Eyckian *St. John the Baptist in a Landscape*." *Bulletin of the Cleveland Museum of Art*, vol. 67, no. 4 (April 1981), pp. 97, 102, and nn. 42, 43, 53, 55, 59.
Lurie argued that if the Philadelphia and Turin paintings are not by one of the Van Eycks, they are clearly dependent upon a lost Eyckian model.

Spantigati, Carlenrica. "Le collezioni di pittura fiamminga e olandese della Galleria Sabauda." In *Per una storia del collezionismo Sabauda: 150° anniversario di istituzione della Galleria Sabauda 1832–1982*. Turin, 1982 (n.p.).
The Turin painting was attributed to Jan van Eyck. It was restored on the occasion of the 150th anniversary of the Galleria Sabauda by Guido and Anna Rosa Nicola in Aramengo (Asti) with the collaboration of Gian Luigi Nicola and Nicola Pisano. The overpaint that obscured the left foot of Leo was removed at that time. No mention of the Philadelphia painting.

Belting, Hans, and Dagmar Eichberger. *Jan van Eyck als Erzähler: Frühe Tafelbilder im Umkreis der New Yorker Doppeltafel*. Worms, 1983 (pp. 159–61).
Argued that the Turin painting must be the primary version, on the grounds of its size, the many *pentimenti*, and the marbleized back of the painting, and that the Philadelphia painting is the replica. Suggested that a third example may have been known in Italy in the fifteenth century.

Castelfranchi Vegas, Liana. *Italia e Fiandra nella pittura del quattrocento*. Milan, 1983 (pp. 67, 71 n. 9, 197).
Following Sterling, Castelfranchi Vegas suggested that the depiction of the rocks of La Verna in the Turin *Saint Francis* provided proof of Jan van Eyck's putative voyage to Italy. She also noted the existence of the Adornes will and the possible connection of the Philadelphia and Turin paintings to it. She noted that Panofsky had doubted the attribution to Van Eyck and that Châtelet had attributed the Philadelphia painting to Hand H of the Turin-Milan Hours.

Silver, Larry. "Fountain and Source: A Rediscovered Eyckian Icon." *Pantheon*, vol. 41 (1983), p. 98.
Silver argued that both the Turin and Philadelphia paintings are Eyckian, although identification of either as the original remains controversial.

Snyder, James. *Northern Renaissance Art: Painting, Sculpture, the Graphic Arts from 1350 to 1575*. New York, 1985 (p. 118).
Attributed the Philadelphia painting to Jan van Eyck late in his career and mentioned the enlarged copy in Turin.

Marani, Pietro C. *Leonardo: Catalogo completo dei dipinti*. Florence, 1989 (pp. 16, 42).
Attributed both the Philadelphia and Turin paintings to Jan van Eyck and noted that the rock formation in the foreground of the *Saint Francis* composition was used by Leonardo in the *Baptism of Christ* in the Uffizi in Florence.

Ragghianti, Licia Collobi. *Dipinti fiamminghi in Italia 1420–1570: Catalogo*. Exh. cat. Bologna, 1990 (pp. 1–2).
Attributed both paintings to Jan van Eyck.

Butler, Marigene H. "An Investigation of Two Paintings of *The Stigmatization of Saint Francis* Thought to Have Been Painted by Jan van Eyck." In *Le Dessin sous-jacent dans la peinture. Colloque VIII, 1989: Dessin sous-jacent et copies*. Ed. Hélène Verougstraete-Marcq and Roger Van Schoute. Louvain-la-Neuve, 1991 (pp. 95–101).
On the basis of technique, Butler affirmed that both the Philadelphia and Turin paintings are Eyckian in character.

Rohlmann, Michael. "Zitate flämischer Landschaftsmotive in florentiner Quattrocentomalerei." In *Italienische Frührenaissance und nordeuropäisches Spätmittelalter: Kunst der frühen Neuzeit im europäischen Zusammenhang*. Ed. Joachim Poeschke. Munich, 1993 (pp. 235–58).
Rohlmann attributed the Turin painting to Jan van Eyck and noted that elements of the landscape were copied on eleven different occasions by artists in Florence in the 1470s, including Botticelli, Verrocchio, Domenico Ghirlandaio, Filippino Lippi, and Biagio d'Antonio. No mention of the Philadelphia painting.

Rosenauer, Artur. "Van Eyck und Italien." In *Italienische Frührenaissance und nordeuropäisches Spätmittelalter: Kunst der frühen Neuzeit im europäischen Zusammenhang*. Ed. Joachim Poeschke. Munich, 1993 (pp. 147–56).
Although Rosenauer called both the Turin and Philadelphia pictures Eyckian and noted that Anselme Adornes owned two pictures by Van Eyck, both depicting images of Saint Francis, he argued that the paintings mentioned in the will cannot be identified with the Philadelphia and Turin pictures since the format of neither picture could accommodate portrait wings.

Philadelphia Museum of Art. *Paintings from Europe and the Americas in the Philadelphia Museum of Art: A Concise Catalogue*. Philadelphia, 1994 (p. 55).
The Philadelphia painting listed as "attributed to Jan van Eyck." No mention of the Turin painting.

Rohlmann, Michael. *Auftragskunst und Sammlerbild: Altniederländische Tafelmalerei im Florenz des Quattrocento*. Alfter, 1994 (pp. 105–10).

Rohlmann listed the many citations of the *Saint Francis* landscape in paintings made in Florence around 1470, and argued on the basis of a detail in the rock formation around the spring in the foreground that the Italians had copied the Turin painting and not the Philadelphia one. Rohlmann ascribed both paintings to Jan van Eyck, but because of the marbleized back on the Turin painting, believed it to have been painted first.

Stroo, Cyriel, and Maurits Smeyers. "Hubert et Jean van Eyck." In *Les Primitifs flamands et leur temps.* Ed. Brigitte de Patoul and Roger Van Schoute. Louvain-la-Neuve, 1994 (pp. 291–92).
The authors noted that the Philadelphia and Turin paintings had recently been reattributed by some scholars to Jan van Eyck without the advancement of any convincing proof. They classified the two paintings as questionable attributions.

Philadelphia Museum of Art. *Handbook of the Collections.* Philadelphia, 1995 (p. 164).
The Philadelphia painting listed as the work of Jan van Eyck.

Van Buren, Anne Hagopian. "Jan van Eyck." In *The Dictionary of Art.* Ed. Jane Turner. 34 vols. London and New York, 1996 (vol. 10, pp. 709, 711).
Mentioned both paintings, referring to the Philadelphia version as a replica and suggesting that it was painted by a member of Jan van Eyck's workshop. Noted that the composition contains an accurate representation of the cliffs at La Verna, and speculated that Jan might have visited the site during one of his foreign journeys.

Van Buren, Anne Hagopian. "The Genesis of the Eyckian Book of Prayers and Masses." In *Heures de Turin–Milan: Inv. No. 47, Museo Civico d'Arte Antica, Torino.* Commentary by Anne Hagopian van Buren, James H. Marrow, and Silvana Pettenati. Lucerne, 1996 (pp. 330–31, 356, 368–69, 377, 386).
Van Buren attributed the Turin painting to Jan van Eyck and called the Philadelphia painting a replica by a member of Jan's workshop, whom she identified as the Master of the Philadelphia Saint Francis.

Index of Works and Artists Cited

Index of Illustrations